29. FEB 00

14. MAY 00

16. APR 02

D1550132

HEARING DOG

Other titles by Angela Locke

MR MULLETT OWNS A CLOUD
SEARCH DOG
SAM & CO: the Heroic Search Dogs of the Fells

HEARING DOG

The Story of Jenny and Connie

Angela Locke

and

Jenny Harmer

SOUVENIR PRESS

611184
MORAY COUNCIL
Department   ical
& Leisure Services
362.42

Copyright © 1997 by Angela Locke and Jenny Harmer

The right of Angela Locke and Jenny Harmer to be identified as
authors of this work has been asserted by them in accordance
with the Copyright, Designs and Patents Act 1988.

First published 1997 by
Souvenir Press Ltd
43 Great Russell Street, London WC1B 3PA
and simultaneously in Canada

All Rights Reserved. No part of this publication
may be reproduced, stored in a retrieval system
or transmitted, in any form or by any means, electronic,
mechanical, photocopying, recording or otherwise
without the prior permission of the Copyright owner.

ISBN 0 285 63400 3

Typeset by Rowland Phototypesetting Ltd
Bury St Edmunds, Suffolk
Printed in Great Britain by
Creative Print and Design Group (Wales), Ebbw Vale

This book is dedicated to
Hearing Dog Connie, and to all the Hearing
Dogs in the UK, for their loving companionship
and service, and to the staff of the charity
Hearing Dogs for Deaf People.

Contents

AUTHORS' NOTE

Throughout most of this book the charity Hearing Dogs for Deaf People is referred to by its former name, Hearing Dogs for the Deaf, as it was known during the period of the events described in these pages. We are of course aware of the change of name and have used it where appropriate, but we felt that for the purposes of historical accuracy the old name should be retained in the context of the time. This also applies to the Royal National Institute for Deaf People, formerly known as the Royal National Institute for the Deaf.

A.L.
J.M.

Acknowledgements

On behalf of Jenny Harmer and myself I would like to thank all those who gave their help in the preparation of this book.

Most especially, my thanks to the charity Hearing Dogs for Deaf People (formerly Hearing Dogs for the Deaf) who have been so generous with their help and support, and in particular to Gillian Lacey, for her enthusiasm and kindness in answering questions and making us so welcome on our visit to the Hearing Dog Centre; and to Director-General Anthony Blunt, for reading the chapter on the history of Hearing Dogs for Deaf People and adding his very useful comments.

I would also like to thank my husband Colin for his help in preparing the chapter on the Cumbria Way, including ferrying me around the fells, and Jenny's husband Geoff and daughter Kerry for help and support. A big thank-you to my secretary Diane Scott, for all the tireless hours of help she gave in the preparation of the final manuscript, and for her superb filing system which enabled the material for the book to be drawn from many different sources.

Many thanks to Sister Denise and Sister Kathleen for their wonderful help, support and encouragement, and for making the journey to Cumbria to meet us on Connie's and Caldey's birthday. I am grateful to them for so generously making available their photographs, and for giving me so much background information on Hearing Dogs. It was of inestimable help.

Angela Locke
Cumbria

Preface

For the profoundly deaf, life is the laughter in the room
which they cannot hear, the joke that nobody bothers to
explain. However high your intelligence—and so often
extraordinary intelligence, insight and awareness may
come alongside profound deafness—if no one explains
who is telling the joke in that crowded room, and you are
not lucky enough to turn and see that person at the right
moment, the sense of laughter all around may be bewildering. I have an image in my mind of my own pupil,
Sophie, quietly slipping away from the crowded table on
Christmas Day when all those shining faces were celebrating a family reunion, and laughter was everywhere. I was
a guest there and suddenly, with that telepathy which had
developed over three years of working together every day,
I felt an empty space. Turning, I saw the vacated place at
the end of the great table and, looking out of the window
at the winter landscape, I saw Sophie crouched by the
family labrador, Maudie, in the cold wind, holding her
close. She looked utterly alone.

In that moment I had a sudden insight, in the way that
not even those three years had given me, of a tiny part of
the world of the profoundly deaf. It is to be for ever
excluded from what hearing people take for granted. It
is never to hear the dawn chorus or the skylark over the
moor or the mewing of the falcon. It is never to hear the
laughter of friends. It is never to hear one's own child cry
in the night. It is never to hear great music, or the sound
of a rushing waterfall, or the wind sighing in the trees.

Once Sophie and I walked together on a summer's

evening through a wood and I suddenly turned to her and said:

'Listen to that owl!'

I could have bitten my tongue! A look of blankness and hurt gave me once again that moment of insight.

For the profoundly deaf, deafness is another, different way of being. We are afraid of that difference and may be uncomfortable with it, because we do not understand, we do not know how to express ourselves. We are suddenly the ones without language. Like seeing somebody recently bereaved in the street, we cross the road because we do not know what to say, or how to communicate. The lack is in us.

So we institutionalise the profoundly deaf. My pupil Sophie had always grown up in the hearing world. It was part of my job to make sure that she was confident to move about in it. She had never, since childhood, met another profoundly deaf person. But when she was eighteen, a friend of mine, owner of a Search Dog whose story I was researching for a book, invited her to a residential school for the profoundly deaf in the south of England. She came back shocked, and shattered. Everyone, she said, wore grey clothes, nobody laughed. The pupils there were turned inwards into a secret, unhappy world, the world that Jenny too experienced as a child at the Royal School for the Deaf in Manchester.

Yet through Sophie, with all her laughter and warmth, and now through writing this book with Jenny and Connie, I have been privileged to see the other world of the deaf. I have sat with Jenny when she was surrounded by her deaf friends in The Snooty Fox; I have been overwhelmed by the gales of laughter which, in a sense, I have been unable to hear because everyone was wildly signing to each other and collapsing in giggles, and I was the one who did not understand. These friends of Jenny have a secret which they wish to share. They are confident in their deafness and the deep richness of the Deaf world is open to them, with all the beauty and subtlety of sign language, lip-reading and those other perceptions which glow when one sense is absent. It is a world of acute intelligence and humour and sensitivity. I have been privileged to touch upon the edge of it, and understand a little of what it may offer.

For Jenny, Connie's gift to her is immeasurably precious. It goes beyond the need to be woken in the morning or to know when the cooker timer has gone off, though that is a vital part of it. There is a far, far greater gift than this. Connie, Jenny's Hearing Dog, has given Jenny back her life, her true identity. Connie has given her the key, and Jenny has unlocked the door. For the first time she knows who she is, and now her life can unfold as it should with all its infinite possibilities. Would that we could all find such understanding of ourselves, to realise our pattern, to be born again, into a new world full of promise . . .

PART 1

Behind a Blank Wall

One

Summer or winter, there is always sound on the fells above
the little Lakeland village of Uldale. The wind in winter
tunnels across the moor, caught between mountain valleys. Then it roars like an express train, but at other times
this wild winter wind has an eerily human sound—'the
old grey ghost', the 'flat bogle' of local legend. In winter
too snow may fall, silently, flake on flake, sometimes block-
ing the tiny road down into that last valley—but even this
white silence paradoxically is a sound in itself, the sound
of the edge of a wilderness which human habitation has
only lightly touched. And in that snowy waste there is
always the call of the raven which nests in those high fells
above the moor, the mewing of the buzzards wheeling in
the white sky, and the distinctive call of the peregrine
falcon, which hunts these bleak wastes for a little sus-
tenance.

In summer the moor is a transformed place, echoing
with evocative sound. There may still be days when wild
rain soughs across the old Roman road, filling its dips and
hollows with huge puddles that reflect the sky, the dykes
bubbling and gurgling with floodwater. Then Swaledale
and Herdwick sheep stand dejected, bleating sadly as they
seek a little shelter behind hillocks the glacier has left
behind. And, as in winter, there is always the sound of
the wind.

Yet on other days there is a touch of magic on those
high moors. The wind dies to a gentle breeze, only heard
as it plays gently among the reeds and the cotton grass
beside the road. Contented sheep-call weaves across the

sunny fellside, and the cry of young lambs seeking their mothers before the summer dusk comes down. The peregrine is here still, squealing as he quarters the moor which is replete now with rich pickings for the young he and his mate are rearing in a nest on the high crag. Here too is the raven, with his 'crark, crark' cry, tumbling in the intense blue sky like a scrap of burnt paper caught by the free wind. And always, always, from Maytime onwards, there is that special sound of high places in Cumbria— the bubbling call of the curlew as it falls towards its nest, wings outstretched, a liquid golden sound over the sunlit moor; the true summer sound of the Lakes.

Stand still in the warm wind and listen . . . for here is the peace of wild places, where sound weaves a continuous tapestry, a peace that is a sound itself, all but lost in our busy world.

If you do not want to risk the wild road across the moor, you can set out for Uldale from the grey country town of Keswick, clustered like an alpine village on the shores of Derwentwater. From there the road runs along the edge of spectacular mountains, reflected in tranquil Bassenthwaite, before turning off towards those scattered villages with their ancient names—Bewaldeth, High Ireby, Ruthwaite—to come in sight of Binsey Fell, overshadowing the inn at Uldale. Binsey, loved by A. E. Wainwright, who described the fell as 'detached and solitary, like a dunce set apart from the class', yet he celebrated its spectacular views over to the distant Coniston Fells and far-off Scafell.

And there, at last, is tiny Uldale, with its white-painted inn, The Snooty Fox. It is hardly on the way to anywhere, especially on those long winter evenings when no one living in these wild fells would venture out unless they had good reason. Yet on many a black night of hail or driving mist on the barren moor above, under those lonely mountains The Snooty Fox is full of folk, its windows glowing with yellow light. Want a good drop of beer, home-brewed in nearby Hesket Newmarket? Wonderful atmosphere, good food provided by mine hostess Jenny Harmer and her husband Geoff, and a traditional fellside welcome? Try The Snooty Fox, over Uldale way . . . It's famous for it.

It is only on a Wednesday night, when you may find the bar full of silent, smiling people, all gesticulating excitedly, that you begin to realise there is something a little different about this Lakeland inn. For Jenny, co-owner of The Snooty Fox, has been profoundly deaf for most of her life, and this is Deaf Awareness Night in the bar, when one can come in and learn signing, touching for a moment the world of the Deaf; a night that attracts deaf people from all over North Cumbria.

And there is another clue to the differentness of this place. Posters of a black dog in a bright yellow jacket adorn the walls, alongside giant blown-up cheques presented by worthy bodies in aid of Hearing Dogs for Deaf People. If you are lucky, the posters will come alive and a gentle black dog, the first Hearing Dog in Cumbria and one of the relatively few, as yet, in this country, will come and put her shiny nose in your lap. Generally, however, one hardly sees Connie away from Jenny's side. After all, who else could tell Jenny when the cooker timer is going off, and when the doorbell is ringing, but Jenny's Hearing Dog?

Those magical sounds of moor and mountain, the call of sheep and the rough cry of the raven, all are a closed world to Jenny, although she has walked the moors above Uldale for many hours, winter and summer. Always with her is her faithful Connie, the constant companion who has shown her the way to a new and equally magical world. It is Connie who has enabled Jenny to make such a success of her life and given her precious independence. For Connie has been Jenny's ears since the day they first set out together into the world . . .

In the beginning it seemed that the odds against Jenny were stacked too heavily; that she might vanish, as had so many before her, into some grey institution, cut off from the hearing world and eventually too afraid to begin making those vital contacts that would enable her to live her life to the full.

We aren't talking about the nineteenth century now, although as you read Jenny's story you might be forgiven for thinking that at times, so cruel was the indifference heaped upon this small girl by the Dickensian institutional mind. To this day she doesn't know who her real parents were. She speculates as we talk—maybe her father was a GI from the nearby American airbase? Maybe her mother, left in difficult circumstances in a less forgiving world, felt the only alternative was adoption. Now, as we write this book, Jenny is gathering courage to try to find out at last, to make some sense of those tantalising clues.

Jenny's adoptive parents had tried for eight years for a child, longing especially for a little girl. Eventually they adopted Jenny and lavished on her all the love that she could have wished for. But nobody guessed that she was deaf. Lack of monitoring in infancy and little awareness of sensory problems in schools meant that nobody was looking for something wrong. 'In any case,' explains Jenny, 'you can't see anything wrong with the deaf.'

Although there were no other children in her adoptive family, her new mother's younger sister, Joan, had two girls—Pamela, a little older than Jenny, and Marian, about three years younger. Their own father died when they were young and the three girls grew very close.

Great Budworth, near Northwich in Cheshire, was where Jenny's adoptive grandparents lived. She has many pleasant memories of visits to their house, and of staying there, and this happy childhood has since provided many of the strengths which have helped her through difficult times. The three cousins enjoyed an idyllic country upbringing, and Jenny remembers the strong bond with her adoptive grandparents. The details of that time remain vivid to this day.

'We children absolutely adored our grandparents. Grandad, who was very strict, had a tall wooden rocking-chair in which he would rock away, smoking his pipe. His smoking paraphernalia was kept nearby on the dining-table which had a dark, thick cloth on it when not in use. Grandma was a small, chubby woman who always sat nearby in a low armchair. Beside her, under the mantel-piece, I remember there hung a doll with an enormous dress in which Grandma kept all her sewing requirements. She was an expert needlewoman and did much sewing for other people to supplement her income. She had an old-fashioned pedal sewing machine. They rarely bought things—even the carpet was made from various scraps of material woven together.

'Everything was very basic. I remember there was no bathroom, just a tin sink in the lean-to attached to the back of the house, a two-up, two-down affair. There was a row of outhouses which consisted of two (rather large) toilets—one Grandparents' and one for next door (which we were forbidden to enter)—and two wash-houses. Very primitive affairs. The toilet was a long wooden bench with a hole cut in it. The bucket underneath was reached by a door at the back of the building. I never saw anyone emptying these! The wash-house had a large brick wash-tub with the means to build a fire underneath and a wooden lid. Washing obviously was a whole day affair— the filling of the tub, the building and lighting of the fire, a long wait for the water to boil, then the action with the dolly-tub. I saw all these often but never saw Grandma washing, as everyone always had to keep out of her way on washing-day.

'There was a tiny garden at the front to spruce the house up and a very long back garden separated into

21

various sections ending in fruit bushes, the whole reached by a long path straight down. At the bottom of the garden the view stretched for miles and Grandad could often be seen down there, scanning the area with his binoculars, looking at Pickmere and Northwich away in the distance.

'I used to stay there every Christmas and on Christmas night we all used to "buck in". Where my grandmother found the room to accommodate us all I'll never know, but I always had the camp-bed, just about the right width for me and so snug, even though I could hardly move in it. They had no trouble getting me to sleep in it, though year after year I vowed to watch for Santa Claus.

'What good times we had! Christmas day we opened our presents, and after the family dinner we spent hours devising entertainments for the adults. Having little in the way of props it all had to come from our imagination. We did a good turn one year when we invented a Mrs Itchy-pants, but we always finished with the song "Irene, Good-night Irene . . ."''

In contrast to this simple country existence, Jenny remembers visiting her Uncle Jack and Aunty Phyllis . . .

'They had a dream garden with a stream running through and a bridge over it. The place always smelt of alyssum, and whenever I smell this, thoughts come flooding back of Uncle Jack. He bred budgerigars. I once asked my mother why they were Uncle and Aunty, and she said it was because they were good friends. Aunty Phyllis died when I was quite young and I remember having my first sad impressions of death. They remembered me every Christmas, and I learnt soon after the death of Uncle Jack, when I was in my late teens, that they were my real grandparents on my natural mother's side.'

Jenny was always getting into mischief. 'During the summer months we would spend hours making matchstick dolls with any leaves and petals we could find—the peony and the antirrhinums were our favourites. The village shop was a fascination too—we could buy loads of sweets for twopence. I remember once, when we went to buy cooking apples for Grandma, I had the basket and as we were going down the cobbled lane home we were all in good spirits and I dropped the apples which went bouncing down the lane. We roared with laughter and I wet myself. I had to wear Grandma's knickers while my own were washed and dried. Grandma's were five sizes too big and had to be secured with a safety-pin! I was a laughing stock.

'I was attracted to trouble, and to water like a duck! The Manchester Ship Canal was a field away on the other side of the road. A heavy stream of large boats would be commuting between Manchester and Liverpool, many from America. We used to look out for these and wave to them, and more often than not they would throw American goodies to us, usually chewing-gum—so much better than ours. It made our day to get these. We were all warned time and time again never to go near those murky waters as they were like a quagmire, but twice I fell in. Both times I was lucky, but not nearly so lucky as the day I fell in the "smelly brook" (so called because it took our sewerage to the Manchester Ship Canal and it smelt like it). There were about six of us playing when I fell in. It was quite some way from my house, too. I felt myself being dragged under and they all just stood there, gaping. No one would help me out, but thank heavens my cries of "Get help!" resulted in one of them rushing off—not to get help from nearby but to fetch my mother. The rest continued to gape and my mother eventually arrived when the water was up to my chin. It took quite something to drag me out, and what a stink!

'Then there was the time when I was playing with the boy next door. They had a very deep hole in the garden, which at that time was covered in ice; it broke when I tried it and whoops! in I went. I would have gone under had the boy next door not held on to the bobble on the top of my hat and kept me afloat whilst calling for help.'

Jenny was always a tomboy and was not very interested in girls' toys, much preferring to be outdoors or, if confined indoors, the next-door boy's Meccano set! But she did have one special friend who became vital to her when things got frightening—a small teddy, her 'laughing teddy' because of the bright sparkle in his eyes. He was her big comfort whenever she went into hospital. For during her early childhood, despite her apparent robustness, her health gave cause for concern. She was always catching things or ending up in hospital with a range of ailments.

'My laughing teddy nearly failed me the time I went in for my appendix operation when I was about seven years old. I had to remain in bed for a whole week after this operation, and after three days a couple of orderlies came up to me with a big jar of ointment which I had seen them administer to the two old ladies on either side of me. I was sure they were making a mistake but they bullied me. This ointment was foul-smelling and, try as I might to smother the smell with Laughing Ted, he wasn't big enough and the smell was too powerful. When I complained to my mother about this, she discovered that it was all to prevent bedsores! At the end of this week I was told to get up, but my legs refused to budge and I had to use my arms to move them. Once on my feet it took all my strength to pull myself forward, and when I looked down at my legs they were covered in spots. It was ages after the operation before I was able to return to school. I did seem to pick up a lot of ailments as a child and caught most things going—I even had pneumonia a couple of times. The only thing that eluded me was mumps. And I seemed to go from one illness to another. Maybe this was the cause of my deafness.'

These, then, were the first frightening memories for a little girl who, unknowingly, was somehow coping as best she could in an increasingly silent world. From the scanty evidence, it seems that Jenny had been at least partially deaf since birth, but now her world was slowly, inexorably, creeping towards total silence without anyone, not even Jenny herself, realising the truth. The situation was mute testament indeed, to the extraordinary intelligence of a child who somehow was managing to improvise communication, so that for a long time no one even guessed.

'I try to remember instances where my deafness was evident. I remember only understanding those close to me—had I become competent at lip-reading, then? But all children take time to understand. Could I, then, have been thought to be a "slow talker"? Even in the midst of nature, as we were at Budworth, I don't recall the sound of birds singing; the sounds of the countryside eluded me. My Grandma had also gone deaf and used to cup her hands over her ears when folk were talking to her, so people invariably shouted—could that have helped me too? Who knows what went on in a small child's mind? Among my early memories of deafness, I remember my mother shouting at me and then becoming quite exasperated at being ignored, thinking I was doing it on purpose . . . Myself feeling puzzled that I didn't hear her . . . Sitting next to the radio and turning it up quite loud in order to hear, and only following the words I was used to and recognised, such as "pip, pip, pip. This is the BBC Home Service—Mrs Dale's Diary" . . . Having to be told when my budgie was talking and what it was saying . . .

'I was taught always to remember my manners—if I made a rude noise I had to say, "Excuse me". On one occasion I said, "Hash Potato", and had to explain to my mother that this was what she always said. So the next time I made a rude noise and said, "Excuse me", my mother said, 'I should say so!'" "There you are," I said, "you just said 'Hash Potato' . . ."

'There were numerous incidents during my pre-

Manchester era (the time before my deafness was discovered) when words fell on my deaf ears. "I've told you two or three times to do this or that!" was quite common, but not the realisation that I hadn't heard.

'Looking back, I fail to understand why nobody took stock of the fact that I only understood when or if I could see the person speaking. Then there were speech incidents. I realise now that even then my speech was poor, always without high notes, as was proved later on my admission to the Mary Hare Grammar School. People gave up correcting me in the end and referred to them as "Jenniferisms", another reference to the idea that I was thought to be a slow learner.'

It might have been expected that as soon as Jenny started school her deafness would be diagnosed, but, like so many deaf children, she had by then become extraordinarily adaptable, and able to function in a hearing world without apparent difficulty, to a quite astonishing degree.

'My first class consisted of all the newcomers, like a sort of nursery—learning through play—and my circle of friends widened to include those from the whole village and beyond. The next class was a bit bigger, I remember, and that was where the teaching process really began and where things began to happen. One day I put my hand up to ask the teacher why she was talking without her voice and was brought to the front of the class. Still unhearing, I cupped my head in my hands and got down to the task of lip-reading!'

At this time Jenny's mother began full-time work at the factory across the road and was no longer there when her daughter came back from school. Now there was no one with whom to share the increasing problems of the day.

'I remember she would leave me a plate of jam sandwiches covered with a basin, ready for when I got in. I managed all right until it was time to move into the top class—I was then about seven years old. It was a large classroom with a big age range, including 11-plus failures.'

Here the problems became more evident as Jenny struggled to keep abreast. The class was run by a strict headmistress rather partial to the cane, as Jenny remembers ruefully, having received 'three strokes of the best' on one occasion. She was also punished for swearing, having lip-read and reproduced words whose meaning and significance were a total mystery to her.

'She punished me when she heard me swearing (I was only experimenting with a word I'd picked up from someone else and had no clue to its meaning) by forcing me to drink a large glass of water into which had been mixed a generous dose of soft soap—ugh! I got punished again and again in this class, which I attribute in part to my not hearing. Talking when we had been told to keep quiet was a favourite. The others would look at me, all of them thinking I was doing it deliberately.'

Jenny was also suffering from tinnitus (noises in the ear) and she remembers one occasion, when she had an intense ringing sound in her ear, when she asked her mother, 'What was that?'

'She said she couldn't hear anything and I realised it was coming from inside my own ears, so I asked her to listen in my ears. I was so sure she would hear it as it was so loud to me.'

It seemed particularly cruel that, deprived of hearing real sounds, Jenny was tormented by imaginary noises so that even her deafness provided no tranquillity.

Eventually, even in that strict and unforgiving environment, it dawned on the teachers that something must be wrong. Jenny's mother was advised to take her to Manchester University and get her tested. They made the journey to see Professor Ewing, and the tests began. Whenever she has had her hearing tested her tinnitus problem seems always to interfere, and she remembers at Manchester hearing lots of noises and thinking she had done well.

Certainly, she decided, she could not be deaf! But then came the shattering news that was to change Jenny's life.

'I spoke to my mother when we got home and was very surprised that I'd been diagnosed as profoundly deaf and was to attend a special boarding-school in Manchester.'

At first this seemed like the beginning of a great new adventure.

'Far from being dismayed, I was actually very thrilled as I'd read books like *Anne of Green Gables* which portrayed an exciting boarding-school life. I went around bragging to everyone that I was deaf and was going to a boarding-school! But I remember noticing that one by one my friends slipped away . . .'

Two

A bus ride, a train ride and a bus ride . . . to the end of the world. Jenny stood in front of the dark building and for the first time began to feel afraid. Looking forward to this day, it had seemed such a great adventure, like something out of the Angela Brazil books about boarding-schools which she had read so avidly. Now, suddenly, it no longer seemed a great adventure . . . not any more.

Before her were two massive black buildings built of huge blocks of stone, forming two sides of a square. There was a forbidding-looking church in the middle, with the Royal School for the Blind on one side and the Royal School for the Deaf on the other, both apparently identical. Tall windows with pale lemon-yellow curtains gave the buildings an even more threatening air. Jenny was suddenly overwhelmed with a terrifying sense that here, before her, was a prison she might never leave.

She clutched at her mother's hand, clinging on to her shreds of courage. Always a plucky child, ready to take on the world with all its challenges, she told herself to look on the bright side. After all, it would be wonderful to have a chance to gain a proper education, with teachers who had a real understanding of the difficulties of deafness. Jenny took a deep breath and followed her mother up the steps.

To this day she remembers every detail of that first morning; it is burnt into her mind for ever. She and her mother were ushered into a room which was well furnished and welcoming, in direct contrast to the grim exterior of the building. There were other similar rooms behind other doors and, peeping in, Jenny thought they looked comfortable and somehow reassuring. Why was it that she felt so afraid? Some deep instinct, some profound unease, stirred in her childish consciousness. Indeed, looking back, she remembers that she was never again to see those rooms at the front of the house, in all the years she stayed at the Royal School for the Deaf. They were a closed world to her, for visitors only.

Her life from then on, once she had said goodbye to her mother, would centre round the enormous, echoing dining-room, the essence of institutional life, with its tables and long benches, and the huge dormitory where the girl pupils slept. After the initial impression of comfortable surroundings, it was a terrible shock, on that first day, to look across the dormitory at the straw mattresses, to smell that faint but unmistakable smell of urine. She remembers gazing in dread at the metal-framed beds in their three rows, with only a chair between to give some sense of privacy. The walls were bare: not a picture, not a photograph, nothing to give a small child some sense of 'home'.

The school was in the heart of Manchester's heavy industrial area and this was reflected in the grimness of the interior. The walls were painted black, with only the cold porcelain in the washrooms, with their rows of basins, to give some light to the prevailing darkness. As she followed her mother through the building, Jenny felt everywhere a sense of that institutional coldness to which she was too young to give a name.

Somehow the feeling of loneliness was increased by the fact that everyone was at their classes, and although Jenny peered through the doors of the small classrooms she couldn't get any impression of what the pupils were like. Still clutching her mother's hand, she went down a large flight of stairs and saw another girl coming up. The girl was smiling but not saying a word, just waving her hands about in the air. It wasn't possible to lip-read her. Jenny stood stock-still and a wave of terror overwhelmed her. She fought back an overpowering urge to run down the stairs and out of the front door, out to the normal world and freedom. But she had been well brought up and knew she shouldn't make a fuss. After all, this was maybe for the best. Her mother, equally apprehensive, squeezed her hand, and Jenny tried to hold in her mind that her parents were making a huge sacrifice to try to give her a chance in the hearing world. She had to be brave.

The tour of inspection continued downstairs into the basement. Here was the 'playroom'. It was bereft of furniture, with forbidding black bars on the windows. Somehow even the air seemed black. On tiptoe Jenny tried to see out, but even beyond the window there was no escape. Between the bars she could glimpse a bare asphalt playground, now full of girls, the whole encased by a high brick wall. It was just like a prison. And for someone who had enjoyed a country childhood, almost worse than anything was that there was not a blade of grass to be seen.

The headmaster explained to Jenny's mother that the walls separated the blind boys' playground from the Deaf School. Jenny gazed intently at his face, desperately trying to lip-read as though her life depended on it, but it was no use. She felt totally cut off, frozen with terror. She had never felt so alone.

Her mother tried to explain to her that she was to go home every weekend, but Jenny hardly paid attention; she was concentrating on trying not to cry, so as not to upset her. But when her mother kissed her goodbye, Jenny remembers, as clearly as though it were yesterday, it seemed like the end of her life, of everything she had loved and cared about. From babyhood she had struggled to understand an increasingly puzzling world, and her adoptive parents, her grandparents and her warm extended adoptive family had been her only security. And

31

now all that was rushing away from her. She was, indeed, alone.

That first night she cried herself to sleep. It was the first of many nights spent in semi-wakefulness and broken-hearted tears. She felt she would never get back home again.

Over the next few years Jenny's childish fears were to be realised. It was the beginning of a black period of her life from which she still bears the scars. This traumatic time planted the seed and now, many years later, one sees its flowering into a strong commitment to ensure that no other deaf children experience what she and her fellow pupils suffered. Jenny sees a powerful need to campaign for Deaf Awareness, to give understanding, compassion and real education to deaf children. Her experiences in Manchester will never leave her. Yet Manchester's Royal School for the Deaf was typical of its time, in many ways reflecting what were still, in the second half of the twentieth century, Victorian attitudes. Indeed, it is hard to imagine that this period was little more than forty years ago. Because of people like Jenny and their tireless campaigning work to bridge that gulf of understanding, much is changing. But as Jenny will tell you passionately, there is much still to be done.

On that first day Jenny lost her identity. She lost her name. That was the worst thing of all.

'That first morning I became a number—223. It was tattooed here, on my arm. I found myself in a totally alien, institutional world. There was marching on the spot in numerical order—1,2,3 to the right, 1,2,3 to the left. It had to be perfect before the pupils were allowed to march to classrooms. There were endless inspections—shoe inspection, clothes inspection, hair inspection, nail inspection. Even for the administering of medicine there was the queue and then the dreaded spoonful of something vile. We regularly had to take a spoonful of senna pods, but, remembering my country lore, I was convinced I was being given lupin pods instead. Such was the climate of fear that it seemed quite logical that I was going to be poisoned . . .'

Even if not poisonous, the senna pods were foul enough. Jenny and her fellow pupils were for ever searching for ways of avoiding taking the dreaded medicine. They rarely succeeded, and over them hung the threat that if they were caught avoiding 'the dose' they would have to take a double measure.

Then there were the fearful hair inspections.

'There was one woman in particular who was very heavy-handed and took a particular dislike to me. She had a small steel-toothed comb and, with my head firmly jammed into a white board, she would plough through my hair. If I had been found to have nits, then I would have had a good dollop of stinking oil poured all over my head. The woman always looked disappointed because she couldn't find anything.'

Playtimes were a tiny gleam of light in those dark days. There were no toys as such and pupils relieved the military-style monotony with full use of their imagination. There was one particular playtime incident that Jenny still remembers:

'The blind boys, on the other side of the high wall, used to play football, and in order that they would know where the ball was it was made of wicker with stones inside, so that it rattled. On this occasion, I remember the wicker ball landing in the middle of a group of deaf children playing in our playground. Such was the sense of isolation that pandemonium broke out and the word quickly spread that the blind were coming! Everyone rushed back into the playroom and the doors were shut, but we were all watching at the windows, knowing we couldn't be seen by the blind children. A small handful of blind pupils braved the enormously high wall and stood in the deaf children's playground, their arms outstretched, asking for their ball. But behind the silent windows we watched, no one daring to go near them. Eventually, after fumbling about, they found their ball and scrambled back over the wall. I still wonder how the blind boys managed to get over the wall when even the deaf couldn't see over it.'

And why, she still asks herself, were the deaf pupils so afraid of the blind? Like strange isolated species they feared each other and were unable, because of that fear, to reach out to one another.

'Even in church everyone kept themselves to themselves and the deaf pupils were in a constant state of terror in case the blind students came near. They never did, but I dread to imagine what would have happened if they had.'

Then there were the much-hated hearing aids, which further marked out the deaf from the rest of the population. First there had been the Medresco Hearing Aid, 'a really bulky thing, hated because it advertised our deafness. We took great pains to conceal it and the leather bag would be hidden under our skirts (we always looked as if we had one hip much larger than the other). The microphone was clipped onto the straps of the bag and hidden under my blouse, but since the controls were on the microphone it was often difficult to be discreet when tuning in. Finally, the headpiece clipped over my head to be hidden unsuccessfully under my hair.'

Then there was the food . . .

'It was so revolting, and the crockery was so chipped and cracked, that even my healthy appetite often rebelled and led me into trouble. I vividly remember one morning being presented with a particularly disgusting helping of bread and milk in a badly chipped bowl. I had become used to the terrible crockery and ceased to notice it too much, but on this occasion the bread was partly green and the milk was almost wholly water, with rancid grease from the bread floating on top. Nothing, absolutely nothing, was going to make me eat it. Along came a teacher who was a very well-endowed woman and, to a small child looking up at her, she was towering. She commanded me to eat the bread and milk, and was quite determined to make me do so, whereas I was equally determined that I wouldn't. She pressed me a little too far and something cracked in me. I threw it all at her from a few inches away and could hardly fail to miss. It was probably quite hot and she reacted alarmingly, and moved with amazing speed for such a large lady. I was terrified, wondering what I was in for. But nothing happened and maybe she realised that I had a point. The meals seemed to get a little better after that and we never had anything quite that bad again.'

But even in this dark world there were highlights. There was Christmas, Jenny remembers, and the tradition of the Christmas Pudding. Many of the boys would go into the kitchens on leaving the deaf school, and these trainees would make the plum puddings. Jenny recalls that they would enter the dining-room one by one in chef's hats, each carrying a plate with their own homemade plum pudding. Everybody would bang their spoons on the table-tops. The cacophony of nearly four hundred pupils banging and screaming for their plum puddings must have been tremendous, but only the staff could hear.

And even being cowed by institutional life didn't stop the young deaf pupils getting up to mischief in the dormitories.

'The three rows of cheap beds whose springs were quite fragile had no hope of surviving the races that were organised to see who could jump on the most beds. Pupils would guard their beds with their lives, because anybody jumping on them was likely to collapse the springs and one would find oneself and one's mattress disappearing down the hole.

'For weeks after arriving, I cried myself to sleep. I was so unhappy and homesick. But at least I could go home for the weekends, unlike so many of the pupils. On Sunday night I would plead tearfully with my mother to persuade her how awful it was, and how I couldn't bear to go back. I couldn't understand how she could leave me in that place, knowing how unhappy I was. Of course my mother was convinced it was for the best, and in those times there were no other real options. Now I realise how it must have wrung her heart to leave me there, so desperately unhappy.'

Jenny remembers that she quite enjoyed the lessons, but the standard was way below her previous schooling, with a great age range. One good thing, however, was that Manchester University was nearby and at this time was in the forefront in providing teachers for the Deaf. These trainees used to come to the school to practise on the pupils, so that there were breaks in the routines from time to time. And, slowly and surely, by clutching at straws, Jenny began to settle in and make some friends. She remembers that among the pupils there were hardly any arguments or fights. They were kept so busy by institutional life that there scarcely seemed to be time.

But much more insidious for her self-confidence than the daily struggle for survival in this institution was the dawning realisation that she was some sort of outcast. Why else was she hidden away? The deaf pupils never left the building and, apart from the university teachers practising on them, the only other human beings they ever saw were the full-time staff. Jenny was lucky that she had an outlet of a warm, loving family, but when she went back home her friends from her early days seemed to have melted away. They had got on with their own lives in the hearing world, while Jenny felt herself to be left behind in isolation.

The institutional life at the school seemed to be designed to make her feel stupid and unimportant—all that marching on the spot, being branded with a number, as if it were some concentration camp. Why did people stare at her when she was out in the 'normal world'? Whenever they heard the word 'deaf' they would beat a hasty retreat, and so often the label 'deaf and dumb' was applied to every deaf child.

'On Saturdays, at the blessed weekends, my mother would go shopping in the town and tug me along too. She'd speak to everyone she knew, and I remember never understanding anything. Many must have shouted when they spoke to me, making me feel even more of an idiot. I became more silent and withdrawn rather than suffer the embarrassment of trying to communicate.

'Holidays became incredibly lonely times for me. I spent them doing jigsaws and my mother would buy me one every Saturday. When I got bored with doing one at a time I used to do two or three together, and then all of them at once, and then I would turn them all over and do them on the reverse side. So under-used was my intelligence that I seemed to be spiralling down into a totally isolated and hopeless existence.'

Jenny's parents always clung to the thought that she might get her hearing back. Her mother had become quite desperate, trudging back and forth to the hospital with her for operations, in the hope that they would restore her daughter's hearing. Jenny would be wheeled into the theatre and a cotton-wool mask put on with openings for her eyes, and the gas was given. Later she would come round to be violently sick. She never knew what, if anything, had been done, and eventually the decision was made to wait until she was older so that they could operate without gas, because it was causing her so many problems. Meanwhile all this kept her hopes alive that one day she might be able to hear again.

Reflecting back, Jenny sees that this non-acceptance of her disability only served to foster her impression that she was a second-class citizen. She felt a total failure and a great burden to her parents. She now realises that they were actually very proud of her, although they were not helped by the patronising attitude of others.

But changes were afoot in this dark world: Jenny would be rescued before she went farther down the spiral of withdrawal, into some empty, pointless existence in which she felt permanently excluded from the outside world.

'When I was about twelve I was called into an empty classroom with another girl. We were seated at two desks and left to deal with a large sheet of questions. Nobody had explained to me what it was about, but obediently I tried to answer the questions as best I could. In fact that was the entrance examination to the Mary Hare Grammar School, the only grammar school for the Deaf in the whole country. Eventually, amid enormous excitement, I learned that I had passed the exam and my parents were asked if they would allow me to go. I realised that anything would be better than where I was, and I was absolutely determined to go.' Now only the oral practical exam separated Jenny from a new life . . .

Three

The day Jenny heard that she had won a place at the Mary Hare was like coming out of a tunnel. It was as though, after years in the dark, she had finally emerged into the sunlight. What a difference! The long driveway leading up to the school, between bushes of colourful rhododendrons, eventually parting to reveal a large lawn covered in daffodils, the whole framing an impressive manor house ... even that first day everything felt new and exciting and fresh.

Jenny and her mother went through a pillared porch into a large room. Jenny remembers fine panelling, a large winding staircase and a marble fireplace. There was an oil painting of Mary Hare, the founder of the school, on the opposite wall. It was as different from the Manchester school as chalk from cheese. That dreaded number, 223, was lost for ever and, symbolically, Jenny got back her full name—she was a real person at last.

Every effort was made to make the deaf pupils feel at home. There were small dormitories, all named after pioneers for the Deaf—Mary Hare, Thomas Arnold, Alexander Graham Bell. There were small classrooms of only ten pupils, with the desks in semi-circles. All of them had audio equipment attached to earplugs with controls, and a microphone for the teacher with a control on her desk in the centre. The classrooms were well lit and cheerful.

'The whole atmosphere was entirely different, full of joy and optimism. The teacher would speak into the microphone and the deaf pupils would tune in their earphones. However, as we were in a semi-circle, with good lighting, we also had total accessibility to lip-reading. All the teachers were trained specialists in their subjects and also in the teaching of the deaf. The huge difference was that the teaching was strongly oral, and the pupils were not allowed to sign.'

The emphasis was on equipping the students for the outside world, although today the particular rule about not signing is hotly disputed in the Deaf world. Jenny now wishes that she had been able to keep up her signing as well as her lip-reading, instead of having to start again in adulthood. If pupils were caught signing they would lose a speech mark and loss of three speech marks meant a detention.

Despite these strictures, the Mary Hare was a perfect boarding-school for Jenny. At last she was able to realise her childhood fantasies—it really was fun. There were even midnight feasts . . .

'We actually got caught once, too. There were about eight of us in it and we had all spent our entire pocket money—2s 6d—on scrumptious cream cakes, the only things that were missing from school menus. We stored all those in one of the girls' suitcases down in the cellar. Someone wagged to matron who immediately removed the locked suitcase to the surgery, intending to open it in the morning. We were all restless that night, thinking about those cakes and the waste of our pocket money. We had a late-night "pow-wow" and decided that we would draw straws and the loser would go down and rescue the feast. Next morning we were all summoned to appear in the surgery where the key was demanded and eventually produced, so that the suitcase could be opened. Matron nearly had a heart attack! All those cream cakes had been replaced with stale bread from the kitchen. That girl was a genius!

'We were all then quizzed as to who had gone down and exchanged the cakes. No one would own up, so we were made to stand in a line in the entrance hall for everyone to eye as they went past. Every fifteen minutes or so the same question was asked again. Other chores were given when we wouldn't own up, so the girl responsible gave in and we all got off with the simple punishment of having to wear school uniform for the whole of the weekend. Chicken-feed, really, and well worth getting the cakes back!'

Itching powder was another hoary old favourite. On one occasion the poor victim was a girl who was busy outside kissing her boyfriend goodnight when the conspirators sprinkled itching powder in her bed.

'She duly began to itch as soon as she got into bed. When matron arrived to order lights out the girl told her of her predicament, saying that she had been rolling on the lawns that had been treated for weed fertiliser. The matron (only a part-time assistant) was quite baffled and went off for the calamine lotion to dab all over the poor girl. She jumped around all night, only realising in the morning that she had been a victim of itching powder. That was not the end of the story. The main culprit was discovered and the remains of the powder sprinkled in her knickers. She was one of the few chosen to attend church for the early service and, since she was late rising, had to rush to catch the car giving them a lift. We saw her set off, looking back in anger and jumping about. She fared worse in church and found it impossible to keep still . . .'

Deaf children, and deaf adults, have a very practical, down-to-earth sense of humour, which can sometimes be rather uncomfortable for the victims.

After the smog of Manchester, the fresh air and plenty of exercise had a wonderful effect on the growing girls, and at last Jenny began to shake off the ill-health that had dogged her for so long. There were even farming activities such as the pig club at the school, in which they owned

41

shares on both a non-working and a working basis, and in which Jenny played a major part. The idea was to get the pupils used to the workings of the investment and business world in a small way, and for its time it was quite a visionary venture. Jenny was keen to work alongside the lads hauling buckets of swill around and mucking out the pig-sties. The enormous boar, which always seemed to be lurking in one corner, caused her some nervousness, but the piglets were a real attraction and Jenny remembers feeding them and getting great pleasure from the contact with animals.

Jenny had always enjoyed sports and games, and when she was small she used to star in the children's running races on the village green. Sport had never featured in the curriculum at the Royal School for the Deaf, but at Mary Hare her love of sports and games came into its own. During the first two years she became a passionate netball player and later took up hockey very successfully. She was encouraged by her father who offered her a shilling for every goal she scored. There was no stopping her. She became quite rich!

In the summer there was athletics, and Jenny became so keen that she trained morning, noon and night, building up her physical fitness. She had good stamina and speed and competed in the 100 metres, 200 metres and 800 metres, preferring the longer distance. Later she entered the area trials, and was frequently the only deaf person in the line-up.

'At first the starting-gun was fired from behind, but eventually someone complained and it was brought to the front so that deaf contestants could see it. It was always a nuisance as it was difficult to get off to a good start. One was constantly having to watch either the starter or one's nearest opponent to follow the "get set—ready" routine. The firing of the gun always made me jump out of my skin because it was fired at the ground and made the earth shake.'

Amazingly, when one considers the difficulties for deaf people in learning their mother tongue, many of the pupils managed to learn a foreign language and gain 'O' level French. Interestingly, French is rather like BSL (British Sign Language) in that the word order is different from English. Jenny remembers the day they had their French oral examination. One by one they filed in to be confronted by the examiner, but were horrified to see that he had a big bushy moustache and a long beard. How on earth were they going to lip-read him? Miraculously they all passed, but it was a real challenge.

Pupils were also taken to the Old Vic to see the Royal Shakespeare Company in action. It was a great day out, Jenny remembers, but she was not sure that any of them actually got the full story. They were even encouraged to listen to music—Gilbert and Sullivan operas and classical music, and dancing was taught to them. It is often difficult for hearing people to understand that the deaf can appreciate music through vibration. After all, Beethoven was deaf.

'When one sense goes the other senses take over and I set a large score by my sensitivity to the vibrations of music. Mother was also very keen on dancing, ballroom in particular, and although my father hated dancing he often went along for mother's enjoyment. Right from a very early age my mother would take me onto the dance floor and I picked up the dances very quickly. Like her, I loved it, and so in due course replaced my reluctant father. She also took me to tap-dancing classes, but apart from the magic little red tap shoes with their bright red bows, I remember little about this although I did get the knack. I feel perhaps that my inability to hear fully led to the rapid end of my attendance at these classes.'

This was a happy time, and Jenny tried to put off thinking what she was going to do when she left school. She tried to live for the day, happy and secure amongst her friends. One thing she did realise, however, was that she was not going to get anywhere with athletics and sport. Her exams had suffered because of her fanatical devotion to sports training, so in her final year she decided to give all her attention to academic work.

The whole enlightened aim of the school was to equip the pupils to enter a wider world, yet they rarely went anywhere alone. Even a trip to the dentist in Newbury was organised to include at least a couple of pupils. The thought of being alone, struggling to compete for work in a hearing world, was a daunting prospect.

But at last the time came when the end of the last school term was in sight. The wonderful years were about to be over, years in which Jenny had felt fulfilled for the first time. She would have to say goodbye to her friends and face that uncertain world outside the gates. She remembers how upset she was at the thought of leaving the Mary Hare. Feelings of worry and insecurity began to surface again. She had no idea what she was going to do with her life.

Four

'I think I was really trying to assess my future possibilities.
I tried going to the deaf club and didn't think it was for
me, but the hearing world quite frankly scared me. I think
this was a result of what had already happened—my loss
of local friends, the intense loneliness of my life at home
and subsequently the formation of an outer shell. It was
all right at school, like one large family, you had courage
to face the world knowing you had support behind you.
Now I was all alone again and the future looked bleak.
All I could do was concentrate on employment and toler-
ate the isolation in between. I couldn't get out to the
pictures or dances or anything. I had no friend or companion to go with and I certainly wasn't going anywhere
with my parents. I formed the idea I would never get
married, yet being an only child I wanted a great big
family. Lots of noise around me, lots of attention. Now it
seemed that was an impossibility.'

While she was still at school Jenny had started writing
off for jobs. She had no clear picture of what she wanted
to do or what might be possible, but eventually she succeeded in getting a job as a work study assistant at British
Aluminium, a short distance from home. This led to a
more senior position in a brewing firm—what would
eventually become the giant Allied Breweries. Jenny really
felt she had at last found a niche where she could be
happy and useful.

'The bosses here were great, even though they didn't
appear to have much deaf awareness. Whilst I was here I
attended college on a day release basis. I achieved my

45

ONC in maths, physics and chemistry—organic, inorganic and physical—and then went on to do HNC in chemistry.'

She was still living at home, however, with all the inevitable tensions. Getting Jenny up in the morning, for instance, became a duel of wits and tempers.

'My mother had adopted other means of attracting my attention in the morning, and her favourite was to flash lights on and off in quick succession. I hated this but it brought a reaction, albeit with a bit of temper.'

Yet home, with all its warmth and safe feelings, was a less frightening place to be than the wider world outside. Away from work she felt cut off from the social life that her workmates took for granted, but she was still apprehensive of too close a contact with the hearing world, with all its terrifying unknowns. However, that was about to change: it was at work, in very unromantic circumstances, that Jenny was to meet her future husband. Shy and nervous of relationships, she was at first very suspicious of any friendly advances.

'I used to arrive early on account of the bus timetable and would immediately set to work on the numerous flies in the lab. I was clocking up an almighty score when I sensed someone's eyes on me and turned to see a boy from Research and Development watching me. He said "Hello" and I babbled something about the number of flies. I was annoyed with him as I was with any boy who spoke to me. We had a lovely lady who was the equipment washer and tea-maker, to whom many of us youngsters went for advice, comfort or just a chat . . . She came to me later and told me this boy wished for a date. I refused to believe her, thinking she was making fun of me, but he had used her as ambassador because he was afraid of rejection and dared not approach me himself. Eventually a date was fixed and I was quite surprised that I enjoyed myself. Our relationship went from strength to strength. We had a long engagement and got married on 1st July, 1967.'

During the time of her courtship she was studying hard for her HNC ... 'I was damned if I was going to do a retake, work full-time and be a housewife, so I put one hundred per cent effort into it which really paid off. I received the Chairman's Prize for the most outstanding results, good publicity and much praise that I had done so well despite being deaf. I never had any problems here at college as I had one-to-one tuition for theory with the tutors. My timetable for theory tutorials was different from everyone else's, but I joined the class for practicals. Since some others who worked with me were also on this course I didn't feel any sort of handicap. It was jolly hard work, though, working full-time, doing all that college work and trying to enjoy my love life.'

Jenny graduated from doing control work to research, happy in the knowledge that her intelligence was being used and recognised. She was to look back on this period of her life as especially happy and fulfilled in career terms, but she now felt it was time to leave work for a while in order to start a family.

'Immediately my deafness came to the fore again. When one is expecting, there are constant visits to the doctor's surgery for monitoring. I always experienced long waits in the waiting-room, much longer than other people, as if they had called my name and I hadn't gone in. I used to tell the receptionist, but never felt they understood. This particular doctor asked me if I had brought my interpreter—I never felt so insulted in all my life. I could understand him quite easily as his lip movement was very clear. I asked him if he could comprehend my speech, which he assured me he could, and I told him I thought his profession should have more understanding. I was quite livid, and the next time I went I barged in saying, "I'm here alone without any interpreter!" I felt that if he couldn't make himself understood, God help us all. Thereafter he appeared a little bit in awe of me, and the topic was never mentioned again. Had I not understood from others that he was supposed to be a brilliant doctor, I'd have gone to someone else.'

Jenny eventually had to have a caesarean operation, which involved another two weeks in hospital after the birth of her son Adrian. She discovered an unexpected benefit from her deafness, as at night the staff would wheel the cots out of the nursery and Jenny was alone in being able to get a good night's sleep. Everyone else could hear the babies crying all night, but she was blissfully unaware.

Nevertheless, the thought that her baby was crying and that she couldn't hear him was very upsetting and the cause of much nervous stress. At least when they eventually got home the new baby seemed to have exhausted all his steam and didn't cry at night, which enabled Jenny to stop worrying for a short while. Both her babies, strangely, seemed to know at once that she couldn't hear and rarely cried.

Even so, her deafness still felt like an enormous handicap after her first baby was born. She felt she needed to be watching him all the time, not only in case he cried but in case she missed any other vital signs of trouble. She would try to sleep close to him, resting her hand on him to feel any reactions. She remembers that it was difficult to relax. She also remembers, with great sadness, that she found it difficult to communicate with her babies when there was no response. Adrian went to school at an earlier age than the other children because they thought he might be slow in developing speech. However, thankfully, he did not seem to show any ill-effects, which is testament to Jenny's and Geoff's loving care. And when her second child, a little girl, Kerry, was born, Jenny felt more at ease.

It was a strange reversal of roles, fighting to bring up her children into a hearing world. Both had normal hearing and Jenny found herself depending on them heavily when she felt they should have been depending on her.

'The children had to wake me when their alarm clock went so that I could get them off to school. When Adrian first started school, when I met him at the end of his school day he would say he was starving and come home to eat like a horse. I wanted to know what he'd had for his dinner since the dinner money was paid at the beginning of the week. He answered, "Nuffink." (I was quite an expert at lip-reading my children and noticed the use of words with letters missing—the "t" as often as not—and also how they quickly picked up the South Derbyshire dialect.) This went on for three days and I thought I'd better investigate the empty plate that he was being given. I duly marched off to the school who were quite pleased to see me as they too had noticed the problem. They then set out to get to the bottom of it. Adrian was getting into the wrong queue, going into the one for the children who brought their own sandwiches. Thank God that was solved, but it quite hurt me that he had been made to suffer. If there were any problems at school the staff were unable to phone me and usually sent another pupil with a note— for instance, if one of them wasn't well, asking me to pick them up. All rather belittling, really . . .'

Inevitably, amid the hurly-burly of normal family life, Jenny, as the only one who could not hear, felt herself excluded to some degree.

'I had little or no say in our choice of TV programmes. I didn't complain as there weren't many with subtitles, especially documentary or live ones, and no one in the family was able to interpret. I often asked and would receive minimal information, and in the end I only asked if it was something I was desperate to know, as my questions prevented them from hearing what was being said.'

Socially, too, her sense of isolation was increasing all the time, and with it a feeling of utter uselessness.

'If there were groups chatting together I'd sit and try to get the gist of the conversation—always difficult and often wrong—so I had to be very careful what I repeated; but I'd sit there regardless, pretending to follow, laughing when everyone else did to be part of the group. I often used to think to myself what a waste of time this was for me, and of all the useful things I could have been doing, but being deaf in a hearing world means that you give up a great deal. You also want to demonstrate a good personality, doing nothing whatsoever that would put shame on your children. You are aware that children can be so forthright, often saying what they think irrespective of the other person's feelings. It will happen inevitably, and you try to build up a cushion for their hurt when it does occur. You aim to make them very proud of you. You hope the hurt will be minimal and that at the end of the day your children will be better as a result.'

Judging by the childhood memories of her daughter Kerry, Jenny succeeded admirably and worried far more than she need have done:

'As a very small child I remember thinking to myself, Why don't Mummy's ears work? But I consoled myself, safe in the knowledge that everyone's mummy was deaf, but daddies can hear.

'It was only later on, when I went to primary school and mistakenly mentioned that my mummy couldn't hear, and that day in the playground I was surrounded by chants of "Kerry's mum's deaf, Kerry's mum's deaf". I realised with complete bewilderment and horror that my mother was different from all the other mothers.

'My first reaction was to be angry at Mother for being deaf and making me different from all the other children. That night I went home with a frown on my face—I was determined to take a long hard look at my mother.

'But what I saw didn't make me angry, or upset, or ashamed; instead it made me proud. I saw a strong, determined, intelligent, funny and happy woman striving to get on with her life amid prejudices from others, who were set on making life so much harder for her.

'Of course, having a deaf mother has meant that I have suffered some losses.

'I wish I could have had those endless mother/daughter conversations across the kitchen, whilst you are both busy doing something, not having to make sure Mum was looking at me, with the light in the right place and keeping conversations to a minimum.

'But mostly I feel proud and grateful because I know that I possess certain qualities that are only there because of my deaf mother. I am a good communicator. I love being with people and making sure people understand what is going on. I know that all disabled people have a voice that must be heard by everyone. I know that I love my mother just the way she is.'

Jenny, however, still looks back with many regrets on the years when she was rearing her children, despite the fact that anyone who knows them sees two very well-adjusted, caring adults who do not seem to have suffered at all. Particularly, she wishes that she had taught them sign language, which would have made life much easier for all of them and would have helped their relationships. Both she and her children realise now how much they missed out by not being able to communicate in this subtle and beautiful language, although they did learn finger-spelling. It is a measure of how little Jenny was able to assert her own view of the world, even to herself, through her lack of self-confidence, that it is only recently these regrets have come to the fore and led her to fight for greater Deaf Awareness.

Meanwhile the dependence and the self-blame continued throughout the children's growing-up. 'I seem to have been far more dependent on my children than I ever was on my husband, possibly because I was with them more and I was, after all, bringing them up. They often had to accompany me in public and just took it upon themselves to explain things, using their own judgement in deciding whether the information was important to me. If someone was talking to me and I knew I couldn't possibly understand them, I could always rely on the children. They also kept me up to date with local happenings. I feel that they were both very aware of my deafness from an early age, and we never had problems with them.

'There were other difficulties in bringing up children and trying to run a house successfully. Suppose someone came to the door? Maybe Geoff would ignore them and they'd go away. If anyone was around they'd answer the door, rarely telling me about it. Often it would be friends of the children and they would make their own decisions about whether it was all right to go out to play, or whether they should invite the other children in. It would quite annoy me, this intrusion into my privacy.

'There were times when I had to call on my children to explain what someone was saying, and often my short, quick replies were roughly interpreted and the children would explain things their way. A three-way conversation, and a distortion of the real thing. After all, they were children, whose way of seeing things was obviously different from that of us adults.'

There are so many little things that parents in the hearing world take for granted, things which Jenny had to deal with in her own way and which often meant developing a tough exterior to shrug off the insensitivities of others.

'All the surrounding neighbours got together and formed a baby-sitting circle, whereby if you sat for someone you gained points and you lost them if someone sat for you. I was in the village shop with a lot of other customers when one of the neighbours shouted out for all to hear, asking if it was I or Geoff who was baby-sitting for her that night. She was disappointed when I said that it was my turn and asked me if I would please wear my hearing aid. I was very annoyed and embarrassed as I always wore my hearing aid then, but my children were never any trouble as opposed to everyone else's, so they all had an easy time.'

After a few years Geoff's job took the family to Stoke-on-Trent, and it was here that Jenny discovered the nearby leisure centre, which became a life-saver. She remembers she made some wonderful friends who gave her a little much needed independence. When she was invited to join the local squash group she found an outlet for her interest in sport and her natural energy, as well as her love of challenge. Nonetheless her deafness was often a handicap, as there were strict marking rules which she couldn't understand. Occasionally she was accused of using her deafness to her advantage and putting her opponent off, although she denies this vehemently.

With the leisure centre came a richer social life: once again Jenny began to feel like a person in her own right. All of us who have brought up children know that feeling of being cut off which comes from being 'somebody's mum' for so many years, in a child's world. For Jenny that feeling had been much worse, and her confidence in herself had taken a real battering.

By now the children were becoming a little more independent and she decided that she was ready for the challenge of going back to work. Despite her attempts to widen her interests through the leisure centre and through making friends, the isolation of home life was beginning to have very negative effects.

'I needed to get out and polish up my act. I was quite convinced attitudes had changed but I was in for a big shock.'

Five

Jenny found herself haunting the Job Centre, but it was a dispiriting time. No one wanted to know, despite her qualifications, and she failed to secure any interviews. In the end, out of desperation, she went along with what the Job Centre proposed: to join a special scheme for disabled people run by Staffordshire County Council, which was their way of helping 'people like her' get back to work.

Part of the contract was that participants should gain more qualifications. Jenny was placed on the public administration course, but no allowance was made for her difficulties. She was not permitted an interpreter, a lip-speaker or even a note-taker, as this would have invalidated the whole idea of proving that she was as capable as the next person of doing a job. Jenny found this a challenging and difficult time. It was an enormous class, with many students studying for promotion. There were discussion groups which were virtually impossible to follow, as were the tutors who turned away from her to look at the board and were always moving around the room. Luckily she found another student who was willing to help her out, letting her copy his notes. She remembers she followed him around like a puppy, desperate to grab whatever notes he had available. She had made up her mind that whatever happened she would prove herself at least equal to the rest.

Jenny now realises that the whole challenge fired up her determination, but at considerable cost. She suffered dreadful migraine attacks after every day at college. The hours were long, starting at 9.00 a.m. and scheduled to finish at 9.00 p.m. 'For me those hours of concentration were ghastly,' Jenny recalls. 'I tried taking deep breaths, willing myself to be calm. And the frustration of seeing other people get away with a poor standard of work, and even being praised for it, was a bitter pill to swallow. It was so easy for them to gain access to the precious information and so hard for me. By the time I had understood that I needed to read such and such a book, the book would long be gone from the library, and yet I really needed those books.' It was a very lonely time and often Jenny almost felt like giving up.

There were other problems too. Once she started work, in the school meals section of the council's Public Administration Department, she found herself in a building eighteen floors up, the highest in Staffordshire. The first time there was a fire drill, she remembers, she was in the toilet. When she came out, the place was deserted.

'I was wondering what had happened when along came the firemen. They gave me strange looks and I told them the problem. People had assumed I could hear this alarm which to them was very loud.'

The building was badly designed for disabled people. The housing section was near the top floor, and although there was a lift which carried disabled people and families with small children in pushchairs, once the fire alarm went off the lifts stopped and the only exit was a metal stairway outside which used to get jammed with people carrying prams and babies, as well as disabled people in wheelchairs. There was total chaos and a chilling indication of what might happen in the event of a real fire.

Eventually Jenny was transferred to Stafford. She was becoming very weary of having to fight battles for the rights of people with disabilities and would have loved to do something more stimulating, but so far nothing else had appeared on the job front. At last, however, a job was advertised in the Highways Department, with the Accident

Prevention Research Section, and she applied successfully. What a different atmosphere!

'The people there had a wonderful attitude. We often all went out at lunchtime, mostly to swim and then to eat, and I was part of it all. Bliss! I'd found something I was enjoying, even though it was a good drive and meant getting up at an unearthly hour.'

This getting up was done at the expense of Geoff who, she remembers, used to nudge her when the alarm clock rang and make sure she left on time. Despite the difficulties, Jenny felt herself very blessed.

'I had a job I enjoyed, with people around me who didn't seem to give a damn that I couldn't hear. I had a home that I loved and was surrounded by my family and I had all the leisure facilities on my doorstep and good friends besides.'

Then came the devastating news that Geoff had been made redundant from Allied Breweries after twenty-five years. It was an enormous shock to the whole family, one that took some time to register with Jenny. However, she threw her efforts behind Geoff to help him analyse his future and what they would do with their lives. He had great experience in all aspects of brewing and he had been managing a large number of public houses for Allied Breweries. It seemed natural to Jenny to encourage him to work for himself.

In the end Geoff settled for buying his own pub with his redundancy money. Sadly, not even Jenny herself felt that she could play an active part in the project. As she says, 'Well, I was deaf. I had no confidence in my own abilities to mix full-time with hearing people, many of whom would be total strangers.' It is hard to believe, looking at Jenny nowadays, with her gift for communication, holding an audience in thrall as she talks about her life, that she was once terrified of meeting strangers face to face. Some new factor must have entered into the equation to change things around.

Geoff went into partnership with another woman who had also been made redundant, thus keeping the woman's touch, an essential aspect of the inn-keeping trade. Now it was time to look for a suitable pub. Ever since the children were small they had spent their holidays on a caravan site in the quiet Welsh village of Llanegryn, not far from Aberdovey. Jenny remembers it was a wonderful place to 'get away from it all'. They had their own van there but no hot water and no electricity.

In 1988 The Peniarth Arms came on the market. Situated near Aberdovey, just outside Tywyn in mid-Wales, it seemed a good place to choose, not only because they loved it but also because they knew the surrounding area well and had friends and contacts there. Geoff began enthusiastically planning for the move. 'It was only when things began to take off,' Jenny says, 'that I sat back and thought, what about me?' She loved her job and her independent life, and after fighting so hard for those things she would find it difficult to give them up. She even thought about getting a flat near to the Accident Research Unit where she was working, to enable her to stay there during the week. It had been such a happy, fulfilling existence for her. However, she felt that her marriage was more important, and such an arrangement would put it under great stress. 'There was no way I could work all week and then trek off to Wales every weekend at a time when Geoff would be most involved in the business. I knew I'd end up working seven days a week and travelling miles as well.'

So it was goodbye to the good life in Stafford, to kind friends in Alsager, to the home they had built together and to the family life they treasured. Jenny was worried about the children. Adrian was often away from home, making a new life for himself, but Kerry was in the middle of studying for her 'A' levels. 'The guilt of subjecting her to this intense disruption at a critical period in her school career was quite overwhelming, but eventually we managed to make a very good arrangement with her best friend so that she could stay in Staffordshire in order to finish her studies.' They were all set to go.

At a time when many families are looking for a more settled existence, Jenny and Geoff went through a major upheaval in their lives in a totally new place, although fortunately not too far from an area which they already loved. But very quickly they found that running a pub in a place where one has fond memories of idyllic holidays, working long hours and trying to manage an independent business, are not the same as relaxing in a holiday caravan—even without hot water and electricity!

Trading began in the new pub, but at first Jenny had great difficulty in adjusting to a world that seemed totally alien.

'It was a sort of return to my life in the Royal School for the Deaf in Manchester—the strong feeling of being somewhere where I just didn't belong, hating the job with its intense pressures, having to go out and meet people, the long, long hours, the lack of real friends because this was my husband's business, and an environment in which I had to depend on other people to keep me in touch with what was happening. Saturdays were the worst days: the pub was open all day, but not for food, so once the lunchtime customers had been served everyone went off to get on with their respective lives. What was I to do? Where was I to go?'

Jenny had always loved animals and found she had a deep empathy with them. Now, when her help in the pub was not required, she began to go for long solitary walks with Blue, Kerry's Red Setter, along the country lanes of Wales.

'Blue and I must have walked every inch of that countryside with only each other's company. I became more and more introverted as the months passed. How I yearned for those years in Alsager, where my deafness had never really stood out, nor seemed to create a discriminating environment. I know discrimination was there, but at the time I felt I wasn't suffering the full impact of it, not like here in Wales. I got on very well with many Welsh people and I respected their language (the region is the strongest Welsh-speaking area in the whole of Wales) as deaf people also have a language of their own, a language that had been suppressed. The Welsh had their own problems too—the influx of English people taking over their countryside and infiltrating their language and culture. I became friendly with younger members of our staff and had a go at learning Welsh, but I soon realised it took all my powers to speak English, never mind Welsh.

'Gone for ever was the peaceful, relaxing family life, to be replaced by full-time social participation, being at the beck and call of customers for long hours, and especially so at weekends. How I missed the happy time when I was pursuing my own career, doing just what I wanted.'

The enforced socialising meant that Jenny was exposed to the constant strain of trying to communicate with other people. She retired to the kitchen for long periods. Getting to know people became excruciatingly painful and she was terrified of social contact.

She also had trouble adapting to her new duties. 'Cooking had never interested me. At the Mary Hare I treated domestic science as a bore and even made a mess of my 'O' level cookery examination by producing a gluey, sticky mass for pastry, which I proceeded to feed into the plughole behind the teacher's back. I had always been glad when Geoff volunteered to do the cooking. So what a change I had to face up to now: I was expected to give my whole attention to feeding huge numbers of people. The logistics alone were intimidating.'

Looking back, Jenny sees that in many ways it was her own sense of self-worth that had suffered, and it was this that made her feel so inadequate. 'That sense of inferiority and loss of self-esteem was growing. Up to now I had been building up my confidence in my own abilities, my qualifications helping me to establish my place in the world. Now I felt somehow subordinate to my husband who I had always maintained was my equal, and to his partner in the business. It was a very hard situation.'

Typically, Jenny took a long, critical look at herself and realised that it was no use moping for what was lost. It was better to get on with the job in hand and do it cheerfully. After that things began to improve as her own attitude changed. She developed some small confidence in what she did, things began to make sense, and there was much laughter to be found in every situation. Jenny has always had a wonderful sense of humour and this now stood her in good stead. There was also the challenge of learning new skills, quite remote from anything she had ever attempted before. The cooking itself, the management and, most of all, the art of working under constant pressure and producing well—all these had to be mastered. The first time she attempted to cook meals for a crowd of people she remembers making the big mistake of looking at the entire list of meal requests on the board and panicking, thinking she would never be able to do them all.

'This in turn made me fumble with what I was doing, totally losing vital concentration, and things got so bad I just had to walk away, feeling an utter failure. Geoff's business partner was a great help in this situation, explaining how to cope by only paying attention to the first three menus on the board. I learned the hard way that it was vital to have a calm approach, and after this I started to get better and began to meet the challenge. But it was hard work, long hours and very few free weekends.

'I started to build up a good working relationship with many of the staff and even got to grips with the idea of being the key leader by using my voice. I learned that it was important to inform everyone exactly what you were doing so that their roles could slot into place. The staff had to watch and be alert to my procedures. Gradually I developed a strong routine and realised how important management systems were for getting meals out at a set rate.'

Determined though she was to succeed in this new life, Jenny still, inside, felt isolated, with no one to turn to who could really understand. The loneliness of being deaf in a hearing world struck her with renewed force, and there were still seemingly insuperable problems to face in her working environment.

'I had to rely on staff to inform me when the cooker timer went off, to avoid burning a batch of cooking. This happened once when I didn't hear the timer. It was a big problem, there always had to be someone around when I did the cooking. Other problems included never knowing if there was someone at the door or if the phone rang. If there were others around they always rushed to answer the door or answer the phone and I was left feeling even more inadequate.

'Many times I felt incredibly lonely. No deaf people ever visited the place, as no one knew I was there. There was a great strain on our marriage as well, for although we were working in close proximity, we were rarely together. At least there were precious times in the afternoons when we had our meals together. I would go to bed at night utterly exhausted and was asleep before Geoff had finished locking up and come upstairs.'

The long walks with Blue continued and were a source of comfort. Jenny struggled to accept what she saw as the pattern for the rest of her life, but it was hard to cope. All her life she had striven to prove that she could attempt anything, irrespective of the fact that she was deaf. She had tried to be recognised as an equal and was a strong believer in equal opportunities and in her rights. And yet here she was, feeling that she was at the bottom of the ladder, her self-esteem in shreds, unable to use her talents. And Blue, her faithful companion on so many walks, was soon to succumb to fits and eventually would have to be put to sleep.

And there was another huge worry, too: Jenny's vestigial hearing was gradually worsening. Over the years she had been able to rely to a certain extent on a hearing aid to help magnify the small amount of sound she was able to hear. Her relationship with her hearing aids since she had first been diagnosed, however, could best be described as love–hate, with the emphasis on the hate! The dreaded Medresco hearing aid, the bane of her life at the Royal School for the Deaf, had eventually been replaced by models with much smaller batteries, becoming less obtrusive as the years passed. But still there had been problems.

'I never enjoyed wearing hearing aids, probably because they aggravated my tinnitus and I was for ever hearing strange noises in my ears. The constant blaring used to make me quite dizzy, and after long periods of wear my ears would also become quite sore. Because I have never heard high notes but have some hearing for low notes which these gadgets magnified, I think their only real use was that they alerted me to the sound source, so that if someone spoke to me I would be cued in to watch that person and would be able to lip-read.

'After getting married I had a great reluctance to wear hearing aids. Geoff preferred me without them, saying I spoke "funny" when I wore them. So they spent long periods in my drawer, only emerging when I went to a concert or church carol service—anything like that where a bit of sound could be a help.'

With typical courage, as her hearing grew worse Jenny privately determined to develop her lip-reading skills to a higher degree, trying not to rely on her hearing aid too much. But it was yet another area of struggle.

At this low point in her life it seemed that it would take more than courage and self-determination to turn things round. It would need a small miracle.

And the small miracle was soon to be on its way . . .

Late one night Jenny, clearing up behind the bar, had been talking to someone about the problems of deafness when, casually, the customer mentioned a charity called Hearing Dogs for the Deaf.

'As far as I can remember,' he said, 'this charity trains dogs to help deaf people in the same way as Guide Dogs for the Blind helps the blind lead an independent life. I'm sorry, I don't really know any more. It's just something I read somewhere, but it might be of some use to you . . .'

Some use! Jenny could have screamed with frustration. Even grilling her informant for ten minutes, lip-reading as though her life depended on it, she still didn't elicit any more information, except that, vaguely, he was almost sure the organisation was based near Oxford. That was enough to begin with: she knew she had to try.

After the pub had closed for the night, Jenny burst out with the exciting news to the family. But the reaction was like a douche of cold water. Concerned, perhaps, that she might be heading for a big disappointment, everyone seemed set on discouraging her. The dogs, if they existed, would 'only be for old people' and, even if there were such a charity, surely she didn't really need a Hearing Dog? After all, wasn't she managing pretty well anyway? Someone really needy, it was pointed out, might be deprived if she were successful.

But no one really knew how Jenny was feeling inside— what it was like to be cut off from so much that everyone else took for granted, or how desperately she needed a special friend, someone who would understand. Jenny was determined, and the discouragement fell upon deaf ears.

'I thought to myself, that is just the thing for me. What I wouldn't get from people I would get from a dog—the companionship that I craved for. This could be supplemented by help with different sounds; it would be the ideal situation for me. My information was vague but still I penned my letter to Hearing Dogs for the Deaf, Oxford, not really expecting it to arrive.'

What exactly was this organisation that had made Jenny prick up her ears, and which was about to have such a profound effect on her life? In order to find out, we need to go back a few years to the time when it all began . . .

Jenny aged two. *Photo: Jenny Harmer*

Jenny (centre) with her cousins Pamela (left) and Marian. *Photo: Jenny Harmer*

The Royal School for the Deaf, Manchester. *Photo: Jenny Harmer*

Jenny aged seven (3rd row, third from left) with her classmates, just before her deafness was diagnosed. *Photo: Jenny Harmer*

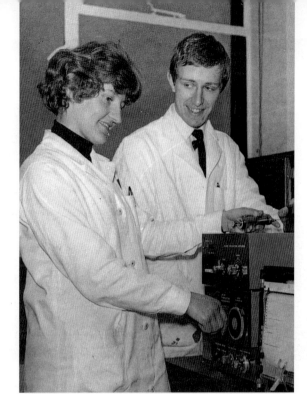

Jenny in the laboratory at Tetley Walkers, Warrington, where she met her future husband, Geoff. *Photo: Jenny Harmer*

Blue, Kerry's Red Setter, who accompanied Jenny on her walks in Wales. *Photo: Jenny Harmer*

Plas Coch, the cottage which Geoff and Jenny bought from Tallylyn Railway and renovated. Their daughter Kerry now lives there. *Photo: Jenny Harmer*

Gillian Lacey, Placement Officer for Hearing Dogs for Deaf People, at the Training Centre in Lewknor. *Photo: Jenny Harmer*

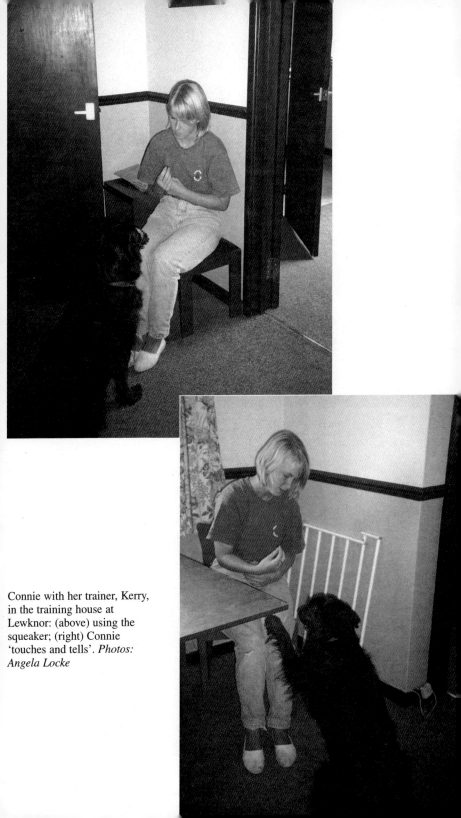

Connie with her trainer, Kerry, in the training house at Lewknor: (above) using the squeaker; (right) Connie 'touches and tells'. *Photos: Angela Locke*

THE TRAINING OF A HEARING DOG

Photos: Angela Locke

The phone rings in the training house. Joy, Hearing Dog in training, responds . . .
. . . and tells the trainer.

A colleague rings the front doorbell.

Joy goes to tell the trainer . . .

. leads her to the source of the sound
What is it, Joy? Show me') . . .

. . . and gets her reward
('Good girl, Joy!').

Connie arrives in Wales. From the first, she loved the country life. *Photo: Jenny Harmer*

Connie's sister Caldey in Bute Park, Cardiff, shortly after going to live with Sister Denise. She is still wearing her probationer's collar. *Photo: Sister Denise*

PART 2

Finding the Door

Six

A skinny white crossbreed with large warm brown eyes stared pleadingly through the wire of one of the kennels, head on one side. He had been picked up by the police a few days earlier, wandering alongside the M4 near Hungerford. Kennel staff estimated he must be about a year old, and had named him Jaffa because of the orange splashes in his white coat. He was obviously in need of a few good meals, and he set to with a will at a big plate of food after being thoroughly checked over by the vet. Apart from being hungry and thin, he was thankfully in excellent health. Now he was the subject of intense scrutiny from a group of humans standing on the other side of the wire. The door was opened and Jaffa, always glad to see people, pushed his inquisitive nose into the pockets of the tall man who was running his hands over him. There was something about this human. He smelt good—kind and reassuring.

One of the women in the party produced a squeaky toy. Jaffa was immediately intrigued. What was going on? Whatever it was, it promised to be interesting.

Pat Reilly was experienced in selecting dogs for the Hearing Ear Dogs Program in America, and was in Britain to pass on her valuable knowledge and experience to the newly formed charity, then called Hearing Dogs for the Deaf. Jaffa seemed alert and interested in the squeaky toy she had produced. Tony Blunt, the tall man with the pockets full of titbits, was an ex-police dog instructor and one of the founders of the Hearing Dog charity. He was watching Jaffa closely. He was impressed by the way the little dog responded so eagerly to sound, keen to investigate all the clicks and rings of the various noises Pat Reilly was producing, seemingly out of nowhere. Head cocked to one side, tail wagging, Jaffa was having fun working it out.

And this little stray obviously loved people. At intervals in the squeaky toy game he would give his paw to anyone in the group, staring up at them with melting eyes full of affection. No one could tell what experiences he had had before he found a home here, but however bad those experiences had been, they had certainly not put him off people. Loving people, being interested in people, and having a great heart were the most important qualities for a Hearing Dog; those, plus intelligence and a natural inquisitiveness.

Pat Reilly pronounced herself satisfied. Jaffa was more than willing to give her a paw—an important signal in Hearing Dog terms—particularly when he received a tasty morsel as a reward! He held them all in a steady gaze and wagged his tail hopefully, almost seeming to sense that his career was in the balance. Both Pat and Tony knew instinctively that this dog was very special, and, after all, the very first Hearing Dog in Britain had to be very special indeed.

Jaffa had passed all the tests with flying colours, and no one could have been more delighted than the dog himself. He quickly made himself at home with Tony and his family and brought a new lease of life to Sam, Tony's retired police dog, as well as giving Anna, the family dachshund, the run around! He was destined to become the charity's very first 'demonstration model', showing the world what could be done.

How had it come about, this charity that was destined to bring support and companionship to so many deaf people? The American 'Hearing Ear' scheme had been the first in the field, and had developed from a single request back in 1976, from the family of a deaf girl wishing to give their daughter greater independence while enabling her to retain a sense of security and companionship. A 'Hearing Dog' seemed the perfect answer. The idea of dogs helping deaf people towards greater independence in their daily lives snowballed under the direction of the American Humane Association and became the American 'Hearing Ear' scheme.

In 1979 veterinary surgeon and writer Dr Bruce Fogle, more recently known for his regular radio phone-ins and for his work as a TV vet, attended an international symposium of SCAS (the Society for Companion Animal Studies) in America. One of the speakers was Professor Lee Bustad, Dean of the School of Veterinary Medicine at Washington State University, and Bruce Fogle was intrigued to hear reference in Professor Bustad's paper to a training programme taking place in various parts of the United States, in which dogs were being taught to help deaf people meet the challenges of the hearing world.

Inspired by this idea, on his return to Britain Bruce contacted Lady Wright of the Royal National Institute for the Deaf. She explained to him that 'deafness is the least understood major disability, that it is financially speaking the most neglected and that often, rather than understanding, deaf people can actually meet ridicule because of their sensory loss'. As a result, she said, there can be tremendous feelings of isolation and loneliness. Lady Wright was aware of the American 'Hearing Ear' schemes, but had felt that there was no way that the deaf charities in Britain would be able to finance the launching of such a scheme, however useful it might be.

Nevertheless, the seed of an idea had been sown, and in 1981 Bruce Fogle and Lady Wright both visited training centres in the United States to look at the work of the 'Hearing Ear' scheme. Eventually, thanks to generous donations from a wide variety of charitable, business and media organisations, a pilot scheme was devised. Free vaccines and medicines were offered and the British Veterinary Association advised its members to treat these dogs as they did guide dogs and to provide free twice-yearly examinations.

From then on the scheme began to take off with amazing speed. In February 1982, at Crufts Dog Show in London, it was officially launched by the deaf actress Elizabeth Quinn, famous for her role in the stage play *Children of a Lesser God*, but the most crucial step for the project's success had been taken before that, when Bruce Fogle appeared on television and appealed to viewers for help.

Among those watching that day were two people who were to play a vital part in the development of Hearing Dogs for Deaf People—police dog handler and trainer Tony Blunt, and audiologist Gillian Lacey. Gillian had been working with deaf and hard of hearing people who were housebound, many of them elderly or disabled. She had become aware of the tremendous isolation that deafness brought with it, and of the vital need for companionship and help. She was also a dog lover and felt that the concept of Hearing Dogs would address many of the problems. Pat Reilly of the American scheme, and Tony Blunt, who was appointed administrator and trainer, set out to find that first, very special 'demonstration model' which eventually turned out to be Jaffa, renamed Favour by the American insurance company Mutual of New York, who put up £2,500 for this first Hearing Dog.

Favour's new star status did not mean that the little dog kept entirely out of mischief. He was an inveterate dustbin addict, which led him to an unfortunate encounter with an empty tin. The scar that resulted from this particular exploit gave him a slightly raffish, if very endearing, air. He also proved to be a bit of an escapologist. On one occasion he was found in someone's garden after traversing unscathed the dual carriageway of the Oxford ring road. If dogs, like cats, have nine lives, Tony Blunt surmised that this little dog was using up his quota rather too fast.

Work on training the first four rescued dogs selected by Tony started from Gillian Lacey's lodgings in the village of Chinnor, Oxfordshire, using Gillian's lounge as an office as there were no official buildings in which to work. The following year, however, they moved to a converted builder's site cabin in the grounds of a local boarding kennels, Forest Glade Kennels. The new charity grew very fast. There was such a demand for Hearing Dogs that at times it was hard to keep up. As they progressed and the real need began to be appreciated, the founders realised that it would be necessary to build their own training centre.

In January 1986 the venture became an independent charity and purchased its first proper centre, a small boarding kennels in three acres of ground at Lewknor, six miles away. Over the following years the site was developed to incorporate two purpose-built training houses, a self-contained flat (to accommodate deaf recipients when they attended for their pre-placement training week), staff quarters, an office block for administration, a fully equipped lecture room, a puppy socialising and assessment building and kennel facilities for up to twenty dogs during their four-to-five-month training period.

In March 1992 the Princess Royal visited the training centre and subsequently agreed to become the organisation's patron. Two years later, following the success of the Touch and Tell Appeal, launched on BBC Television in 1991, another training facility, the Beatrice Wright Training Centre (named after the organisation's co-founder, Lady Wright), was opened in the village of Cliffe near Selby, North Yorkshire.

From the beginning, following Jaffa/Favour's example which had proved so successful, most of the dogs used were from rescue centres such as the National Canine Defence League. This meant that dogs who, through no fault of their own, had been relegated to the canine 'scrap heap', living out their lives in rescue kennels if they were lucky or, if they were unlucky, having to be put to sleep, now had the chance to make the most of their intelligence, playing a really useful role in a relationship with a deaf person. These dogs were most likely to be cross-breeds, ranging in size from small to medium, and could be male or female, aged between six weeks and three years.

Today people often remark on the wonderful diversity of dogs which are used as Hearing Dogs. Unlike Guide Dogs for the Blind, or Search Dogs, these are not always large Labrador or Retriever-type dogs (Connie is almost an exception to the rule). There could be almost anything at the end of that lead! Why do Hearing Dogs use such an amazing pot-pourri of breeds? Fundamentally, unlike Search Dogs or Guide Dogs, the tasks the dogs perform don't really need any particular physical stature. They don't have to guide people physically or pick up large items or jump over high obstacles. They don't have to track scents over long distances, leap over stone walls or make their way across dangerous mountain crags. Their work is very subtle, and involves responding to sounds, touching people and leading them to sound sources. A dog of any size can do this, provided it is normal, fit and healthy, with sufficient mental agility to perform its task well.

Consequently, Hearing Dogs are able to select dogs from a wide variety of sources—rescue centres, donated dogs from breeders, or unwanted pets from members of the public. Not only large dogs, who have been traditionally associated with useful, dependable characteristics, but also tiny dogs such as Papillons, Chihuahuas, Lhasa Apsos, Cavalier King Charles Spaniels and Yorkshire Terriers can play their part. There is even one Chinese Crested x Japanese Chin whose owner has an allergy to dog hair—this virtually hairless dog is a real gift from heaven for her grateful owner. Elderly owners are particularly glad to have a tiny breed which requires much less exercise than a gundog or working dog.

Nevertheless, it still comes as a surprise to see a Toy Dog with a miniature yellow jacket proclaiming 'Hearing Dog for Deaf People'. The charity's coat manufacturer has had to expand his range of sizes from the standard small, medium and large, and now frequently makes extra small and extra, extra small sizes. So don't be surprised if you come upon that distinctive yellow jacket one day on a large Labrador and the next on a miniature Pinscher. They are all doing a wonderful job.

Favour, that very first hearing dog, had won hearts all over the country. By demonstrating the work of Hearing Dogs to the public with Tony Blunt as his trainer, the little orange and white dog was a real contributory factor in the nationwide success of the charity. Favour became a familiar 'media star' and appeared on many TV shows.

Sadly, his career almost came to a tragic end. It was Christmas 1990 and the staff were preparing for their first television appeal for a second training centre. Tony Blunt was taking Favour on his usual nightly walk across the fields when suddenly another dog appeared from nowhere and attacked Favour, who disappeared into the blackness, yelping in fear and terror. Tony searched for him for over an hour before finally his torch picked out a flash of white fur in a roadside ditch. Little Favour was lying in the mud, apparently lifeless, and Tony saw with horror that he had suffered a knock on his head.

Christmas that year was a worrying and unhappy time for the Blunt family. It was testament to Favour's nine lives, and to the loving care lavished on him by the Blunts, that the little dog survived at all. There seemed to be possible damage to his back legs, and his recovery was long and slow. It was several months before he was well enough to go back to his beloved demonstrations.

With increasing rheumatism, perhaps as the result of his accident, he became slower and slower and was eventually given an honourable retirement. Hearing Dogs had now been in existence for almost a dog's lifetime, years during which Favour and his colleagues had literally become 'friends in deed' to more than 178 deaf people throughout the United Kingdom. A special parade at Crufts Dog Show in 1993 honoured the career of that little orange and white dog whose great heart and willingness to learn had been the beginning of a lifeline for so many. A certificate of service for his devotion to duty over all those years spoke volumes for everyone involved in Hearing Dogs for the Deaf.

Seven

By the time Jenny learned about Hearing Dogs, from that chance remark in the bar of The Peniarth Arms, the charity was well established in its headquarters in Lewknor. Despite the vague address of 'Hearing Dogs for the Deaf, Oxford', Jenny's first letter successfully reached its destination.

She was on fire with anticipation while she waited for a reply, although she told herself it was foolish to hope for something that seemed so out of reach. Still, she could not help hoping. How wonderful it would be to have the companionship of a dog of her own, who would not only be a friend, but would also enable her to have precious independence.

Jenny's long walks with Kerry's Red Setter, Blue, had helped her through a difficult period, and all her life animals had given her that unquestioning, telepathic friendship which was balm to her sense of isolation.

'We had a small mongrel, Penny, whom I was devoted to,' she remembers of her childhood. 'She would bark furiously when anyone knocked at the door. I'd often refuse to answer and would try to slip upstairs and look to see who it was, only running out to catch them if I felt at ease with them. All my life I loved animals. They provided me with companionship, trust and love, and accepted me despite my deafness—all the things lacking in many human beings—and so I turned to animals and shared their world. I would, given the chance, have taken in every waif and stray that came my way but my father had a deep allergy to furry things. The dog he accepted but he never stroked it; cats were quite out of the question and were forbidden. The goldfish and the budgie were all right. I did have a beautiful all-white guinea pig which had to be kept outside, especially after it ran up my father's trouser leg, but that's another story . . .'

Meanwhile Hearing Dogs had been busy on her behalf and things were beginning to fall into place.

'The morning the letter arrived from Hearing Dogs for the Deaf, along with an application form and a request for a recent audiogram, was the start of major changes in my life, though I didn't realise it at the time.

'I made an appointment for an audiogram and I was amazed when I received it—just one small wire connecting the two frequencies at the bottom of the graph. There was no disputing my deafness. I duly filled in the application form, all the while receiving negative responses from Geoff, who I think wanted to be sure I was making the right decision and also had the realisation that he would be losing some of his responsibilities. I'm not sure he was ready to accept all that.'

Jenny sent off her application and there followed the second agonising wait. Then came the morning when she had a letter telling her that Tony Blunt was coming to visit her for an assessment. All Jenny knew was that he was a former police dog instructor, was a founder of Hearing Dogs for the Deaf and was now its Director-General. It was enough to make her very nervous. After all, she still felt like an imposter. Even that audiogram, which showed so clearly that she was in fact much deafer than she had realised, failed to convince her. Somehow, despite increasing deafness and isolation, she had always struggled on. She couldn't imagine that she would have a chance to qualify for a Hearing Dog.

Thus, when this tall, imposing man ducked in through the door of The Peniarth Arms, Jenny was in a real state of nerves; her knees were literally shaking. He was so tall and, frankly, a bit intimidating, like an army officer. But the Director-General of Hearing Dogs, despite appearances, proved to be kindness itself, listening with close attention as Jenny explained about her life and the challenges she faced every day. Very soon she began to feel more at ease. She took him round the pub to show him the working conditions, and to explain all her particular difficulties. It was a relief, somehow, just to be able to talk to someone who really seemed to understand.

Afterwards they made the journey up to Plas Coch, the beautiful but isolated cottage in the mountains which Jenny and Geoff had bought from the Tallylyn Railway, and which they were occupying part-time while renovating it. This isolation was also imposing its own set of challenges for a deaf person.

'I was trying to convince Tony of my need for a Hearing Dog, and being so much in awe of him I was really strung up. Our circumstances were a bit strange as until the renovations were completed we didn't have any independent living facilities. He questioned me on everyday living and what I needed the dog to do for me, and we went to visit the site of the cottage for him to see the isolated spot. As Geoff would have to spend a large amount of his time at the pub I would live at the cottage for a great deal of the time on my own.'

Tony explained that the guidelines for Hearing Dog applicants were that the applicant must have a severe, profound or total hearing loss, and thus a real need for a Hearing Dog. This would include help with sounds such as the alarm clock, doorbell, telephone and smoke alarm. And it was really important that the potential recipient should be physically and financially able to care for the dog. That meant providing exercise and grooming, the right food and medical care.

'You know,' he said gravely, as they walked down the path from the cottage, 'a Hearing Dog is not a machine.

77

It's a living, breathing creature who also needs love and reassurance, as well as the best care you can give it. Bear in mind that this is a very tiring profession for a dog, often stressful and with long hours. After all, the animal has to be awake in the morning before the handler, and is only ''off duty'' when she or he goes to bed. Even then the dog must stay alert for the unexpected—a smoke alarm, for example. So sympathetic care and a great deal of love are very important.'

As Blue, by now rather stiff and frail, walked slowly ahead of them, Tony stopped for a moment. 'By rights, Hearing Dogs shouldn't really go to homes where there are other dogs. It is too difficult for the bonding process.' Jenny shook her head and explained sadly that Blue was in fact very old now and not expected to live long.

He nodded. 'You'll miss her companionship, won't you? From what you've said, you've had some great walks together and she's been a real friend. That's how it should be. We look for people who genuinely seek the close companionship of a dog and want to form a working partnership with one. It's a hard thing to define.'

Jenny, lip-reading with absolute concentration, nodded enthusiastically.

'That's definitely me,' she said firmly. 'There is nothing I would love more than to have a companion like that. Blue has been a wonderful friend to me, even though she really belongs to Kerry. I shall miss her so much when she's gone. And ever since I first heard about the Hearing Dog scheme, I realised that such a special dog could always be here for me, when I feel most alone and vulnerable. I knew that was exactly what I needed, from that first moment. And,' she laughed, 'of course it works both ways. I would always be here for him, or her. I've always loved dogs, anyway.'

Tony listened gravely.

'You know, running a pub would be a very unusual

environment for a Hearing Dog. It would need a great deal of thought in training for those needs. And I can see that you would also be spending a lot of time alone. That has its own problems, hasn't it? Two very different sets of challenges—total isolation, and an environment which could hardly be more hectic, stressful or full of people. Quite a lot for one dog to take on board.'

He paused. 'If your application were successful'— Jenny's heart beat faster and she tried not to look too excited—'from what I have seen today, it seems you would need the dog to work with you in what are basically two different "home" environments ... Mmmm ...' He looked thoughtful. 'Perhaps it could be done. We at Hearing Dogs always like a challenge!'

Courteous as ever, he shook hands gravely and ducked his head once more through the doorway of The Peniarth Arms.

'I'll go back now and write my report. Don't worry. I'll get back to you as soon as possible. You'll certainly be hearing from us soon, one way or the other.'

Jenny tried to calm down as she said goodbye. What did it all mean? Could there really be a chance that she might get a Hearing Dog? She was left both elated and depressed. Had she given a good account of herself or had she completely messed it up? How on earth was she going to wait without going totally mad?

The next few weeks seemed endless. Over and over again she went through her interview with Tony Blunt. Had she given the right answers to his questions? Hearing Dogs cost a lot of money to train, didn't they? There must be so many other people out there with a crying need for a Hearing Dog. A greater need than hers, she was sure. No, it wasn't even worth hoping. It would be too much like good luck actually to be awarded such a prize—like winning a Gold Medal in the Olympics, something to be dreamt about but never entertained seriously. Geoff had been right: there must be far more needy people around. She really couldn't be among the most deserving . . .

She tried to be firm with herself and suppress any stray hopes that she still had. Yet every once in a while the vision of a Hearing Dog of her own stubbornly leaped into her mind and she found herself excited all over again.

Then came the fateful day: the red post van climbing the track to the cottage, as close as it could get, the post-man getting out with a bundle of letters. She rushed to the gate, as she had every morning since Tony Blunt's visit.

It was a beautiful summer's day. The postman was in no hurry to get back into his van. It was going to be hot, wasn't it? He was fed up with being cooped up in the van. He would rather be in his garden. Jenny had spied the Hearing Dog logo on the envelope and was burning up with impatience, but it was several minutes before she was able to tear herself away from the gossip of the valley and hurry into the kitchen, opening the letter with shaking fingers. Yes! No! In a moment she would know for certain. Her future was in that small white envelope.

Dear Mrs Harmer,
We are pleased to inform you that your application for a Hearing Dog has been accepted.

Could you please keep us informed of the progress with the cottage.

We look forward to hearing from you.
Yours sincerely,
A. G. Blunt
Director-General
Hearing Dogs for the Deaf

'So I must have passed the test . . . The waiting—and the dreaming!—began . . .'

Eight

Later that year, in December 1991, a litter was born to a Golden Retriever father and a Collie mother, a wonderful combination of gentleness, intelligence and strength. The temperament of these puppies was to be proved twice over after the whole litter had been donated to Hearing Dogs for the Deaf, in that not just one but two of the puppies were selected for training as Hearing Dogs. Connie and Goldie, as her sister was known at first (her name would be changed later to Caldey), were beautiful puppies, almost all black, but with a ripple of gold in their coats and golden tufts in their paws. In many ways they both resembled Flatcoat Retrievers, and could have been taken for that breed had it not been for that magical golden light in their fur. The Golden Retriever/Collie cross is renowned for its stability of temperament and affectionate nature. Both breeds are used with great success as Mountain Rescue Search Dogs, especially the Collie with its stamina and intelligence, and the Collie is a perfect working and trialling dog. Golden Retrievers are used widely as working dogs, and, particularly indicative of their gentle intelligence, alongside Labradors as Guide Dogs for the Blind.

In short, it would have been hard to breed a better combination of temperament, stability, gentleness, willingness and a loving nature—all perfect qualities for a Hearing Dog. And so it was to prove in the months to come when the two dogs began their training.

Connie and Caldey, at eight weeks old, were immediately placed in separate home situations, each with their own socialiser. This important 'link in the chain' would

81

be responsible for preparing the two young puppies for every aspect of daily life in a normal home. Dogs accepted into the Hearing Dogs training scheme vary in age, from as young as six weeks up to about three years old. All are unwanted or donated, and most are passed straight to a puppy socialiser from a rescue centre or from their previous home. The charity provides food, toys, bowls and all necessary equipment for each dog and keeps strict tabs on how the puppy is progressing.

Connie's socialiser, Christine, has many happy memories of her time with Connie. Like all socialisers recruited by Hearing Dogs, she is a volunteer worker who takes young dogs for periods of from two to eight months, depending on the dog's age and previous experience in a home.

With Connie as a young puppy, coming straight from her mother, it was a case of starting from scratch. This meant beginning with the all-important house training, progressing to walking on a lead, getting her used to everyday occurrences, meeting people of every shape and size, including babies and children, and attending obedience classes. Connie proved herself a willing and intelligent pupil, with a truly gentle nature. Christine was asked to take Connie on public transport, in cars where possible, and into public places once her inoculations were complete. She had to be unfazed by anything, from heavy lorries thundering along six inches from her ear, to noisy crowds in a shopping arcade.

Any lack of confidence at this stage would have made future training very difficult and would have put a question mark over the suitability of Connie as a potential Hearing Dog. As the socialising manual, loaned to all socialisers for day-to-day guidance, points out, this early education in impeccable manners, good behaviour and acceptance of all situations is essential to the dog's future training as a Hearing Dog for a deaf person.

Jenny explains:

'She was introduced to all the situations she would be expected to cope with and would meet in later life. The dogs accompany us everywhere so must be reliable in all situations. All the time Christine was assessing Connie's capabilities to see if she was suitable to be a Hearing Dog. She was introduced to traffic, buses, trains and met lots and lots of people and was taken on public trips to places like schools and shops. This socialising enables the centre to form a fuller picture of the dog's temperament and previous life and assists in matching the right dog to the right person.'

Indeed, Connie's excellent early training has been proved over and over again, as she must surely have one of the most socially interactive jobs around for a Hearing Dog. She passed out from those vital early months of training with flying colours and, despite her gentle submissive nature, showed confidence in every kind of everyday situation. Her file from that time notes that she was a friendly dog, although rather shy with strangers, that she loved children, was confident, and was 'submissive to other dogs'. The assessment noted too that she had been worried by 'something flapping in the wind', that there was 'no problem taking bones off her', that she was 'quite excitable in the training centre', had 'good reaction to sound' and, very important, that she was obedient.

Altogether a very good assessment, although a note was made to work on her reaction to strangers. Overall, her trainer Kerry remembers, Connie was bright and keen to work. One note on the file of this otherwise almost perfect dog, that 'she travelled well in the van', might come as a bit of a surprise to those who know and love her today. This relaxed attitude to travelling in a car or van seems to have worn off, as Jenny will tell you, and I too have vivid memories of trying to persuade Connie to travel in the back of my Volvo estate when Jenny and I drove down to Lewknor while working on this book.

I had carefully put all the cases on the back seat and left the rear space of the estate entirely free for Connie—or so I thought! Jenny carefully removed a large stone which my dogs had left there and which might roll around, my umbrella, wellington boots and all the other clutter I had ignored through familiarity.

With much coaxing we encouraged Connie to get in the back, but within seconds there was trouble. She didn't like the back of the car and began to push herself through at one side of the dog guard into the back seat, a determined expression on her face.

We watched helplessly, and she was quite immune to our entreaties. Eventually she was almost through except for her back legs. She lay on top of the cases in the back seat looking most uncomfortable, her tail and back legs still stuck in the boot. One by one we moved the cases into the boot of the car and all the bits and pieces—Jenny's briefcase, my camera equipment and all the stuff Jenny had already moved! Reluctantly Connie was persuaded to sit up in the back seat, like a queen!

After the initial assessment at Lewknor, it was time for Kerry and Claire Guest, the training manager, to make that all-important decision, and to match a potential recipient with Connie. Jenny's file was studied, along with other potential owners. It was a big decision, and many factors had to be taken into consideration. A mismatching at this stage could be deeply traumatic and unsettling for both sides in such a delicately-balanced partnership. What would Jenny's needs be, and would Connie be the right dog for her?

In the meantime other things were happening in Jenny's life which made the acquisition of a Hearing Dog even more important. The first was her own realisation that she was more than capable of running a pub. By now she had acquired a minicom, a machine whereby the caller can type onto the screen linked to a phone and this can be read at the other end by the recipient, who can then type a reply if he or she also has a machine. This was a revolutionary step forward for Jenny. Apart from the precious human contact which enabled her to keep in touch with family and friends, with a minicom and 'type-talk' (in which an operator is the link), and, later, with a fax machine, she would be able to conduct all the business of the pub so much more easily.

Looking back, Jenny realises that all the time she was in Wales, helping out at The Peniarth Arms, she had kept her wits about her learning the ins and outs of running a public house, especially the catering and book-keeping. She was now pretty expert at both and felt she could do it on her own as Geoff's full business partner.

So Jenny and Geoff decided it was time they went into business together and started to look ahead. They finally settled on the Lake District for their new venture. They had many happy memories of holidays there, and of the beauty of the mountains.

'When we were at The Peniarth Arms we used to take our holidays in a rented cottage in Keswick. And just as we used to holiday in Wales before we moved there, the Lakes became our second home. When we went into partnership ourselves it was therefore quite natural that we should want to settle in the Lake District.'

Living there, they reasoned, would give them wide access to the tourist trade, and they would be in beautiful surroundings in mountains and unspoilt countryside which they both loved. They resolved to start looking.

'We scoured hundreds and hundreds of information sheets sent by the estate agents, and I liked The Snooty Fox straight away.' When Jenny and Geoff went to see it for the first time, they fell completely in love with it. Nestling in the tiny village of Uldale, the little white-painted inn, so cosy and welcoming in the fold of the fells, seemed exactly right. The area was reminiscent of Wales but had some added magical quality. Jenny was sure she would be happy there, but the price was quite impossible.

Resolutely they put it out of their minds. It seemed as though they would just have to go on looking.

During this time the health of Jenny's mother had deteriorated. Sadly, she had developed ovarian cancer. Jenny brought her home in order to look after her and has a last happy memory of pushing her around Derwent-water on a visit to the Lake District. Her mother, Jenny remembers, loved it. But if they wanted to talk to one another and share the beauties of that magical lake, set in its spectacular cradle of mountains, they could only do so if, every time, Jenny stopped the wheelchair, put on the brake, and came round to face her mother so that she could lip-read and respond.

'My deepest regret was that she never learned to sign. She came to me that November, while we were still in Wales, and I nursed her. She needed small meals many times a day so I was running up and down stairs like a yo-yo. Prior to her death she was very ill. She removed her teeth and was practically impossible to lip-read, so during her last days there was no communication between us. It would have been great to be able to talk together with our hands to express our feelings. I have never liked to talk to anyone when I knew I wouldn't get a response.'

In December 1991, while Jenny was holding her mother, she died in her arms. Jenny felt utterly bereft.

'That wonderful woman, who had done her best for me, looked after me and loved me all those years, was now gone from my life. I was devastated. My grief was paramount, much more so than after the death of my father.'

This loss, combined with all the new challenges on the horizon, made Jenny even more aware of her need for a friend, a confidant, someone special to love when she felt alone. Yet time was passing, month after month. It had been July 1991 when Jenny had first heard the news that she was eligible for a Hearing Dog. Since then she had thrown herself wholeheartedly into raising funds for the charity. It had been a way of doing something, a sense of satisfaction to know that someone, somewhere, was being helped. But for herself, she still couldn't help thinking and hoping that maybe, soon, it might be her turn. It had been well over a year, and was now the winter of 1992. She was beginning to feel desperate. Had she been forgotten? Around this time Blue, who had been such a faithful companion and was now very frail, began to have increasingly severe fits and had to be put to sleep, much to the whole family's distress.

'I had lost four members of my family, including my mother and our Red Setter, Blue. I felt all my loved ones were leaving me and the loneliness was beginning to set in. The old days of "walkies" had gone and I felt disinclined to go walking alone. All the memories of Blue would come gushing back when I did. I was beginning to feel quite unfit. I was still waiting for my Hearing Dog but beginning to give up now, thinking that the decision to allow me to have a dog had been reversed. I was really considering the idea of visiting a dogs' home, and maybe trying to train a dog to my own requirements, even though I realised this would be a long and difficult task. I felt I was losing my independence and was beginning to worry about staying in alone on account of the doorbell and the phone.'

November: the darkest days of the winter. That familiar sense of loneliness, of being shut in on dark evenings, of the isolation which life in a remote Welsh valley can bring, even for a hearing person. Somehow, the bustle of the pub made that loneliness, that sense of being cut off, so much worse.

Suddenly, out of the blue, they heard that the price of The Snooty Fox had tumbled dramatically, and they realised that it was within their grasp. They could hardly believe it. Within a few days their offer was accepted. They were on their way to owning their dream pub, a pub which Jenny and Geoff would share and run as real partners. Perhaps, after all, there was a light at the end of the tunnel . . .

Then came November 23rd. A Monday morning. A rare, bright winter day. The mountains sharp in the frosty air, last brown leaves on the hedgerows. A sense maybe of the ends of things, maybe a promise of new beginnings—a new business, a new partnership with Geoff . . . and perhaps another new partnership which would change everything. A letter brought up the winding road to Plas Coch: another letter with the Hearing Dog logo on the envelope.

Dear Mrs Harmer,

I am writing to offer you 'Connie'—see photo enclosed—a medium-sized Golden Retriever x Collie, 10 months old, spayed bitch. I would be very grateful if you could come and visit Connie at the Training Centre, so that you can meet each other and so that we can discuss final plans for sounds, etc. Please let us know when you are able to visit.

We look forward to meeting you.

Yours sincerely,
Claire Guest
Training Manager
Hearing Dogs for the Deaf

That new life was about to begin. The two of them were about to meet for the first time . . . the small miracle was on its way.

Nine

Jenny's diary notes:

First news of 'Connie'—elated, had been thinking
about the need for a dog and thought my application
for a 'Hearing Dog' had been reversed on account
of our changed circumstances. Then on Nov 23rd
the letter arrived ... and a photograph. She is
beautiful!

By now Geoff had sold his partnership in The Peniarth
Arms and their plans for their new business in the Lake
District were going full steam ahead. Meanwhile they were
both living at Plas Coch.

At the end of November Jenny drove down to Win-
chester to spend the weekend with her best friend, Davina,
who had been at the Mary Hare Grammar School with
her. They spent a happy weekend reminiscing about old
friends and catching up on gossip. Davina's family had
been especially kind to her when she was a pupil at the
Mary Hare and was unable to get home for weekends,
making her very welcome in their own home. Since then
the two of them had maintained a strongly supportive
relationship.

Monday morning dawned black and wild, with a gale
blowing and torrential rain. Hardly auspicious weather!
The roads were flooded inches deep as Jenny struggled
to drive to the Hearing Dog Centre at Lewknor, peering
through the windscreen at the lashing rain.

Despite the weather she was in a state of high anticipation. Would it be love at first sight, or a real disaster? She tried to imagine what Connie would be like. She had looked at her photograph over and over again, examining every detail. It was so frustrating, trying to imagine. Physical appearance was one thing, but the reality? Would she be gentle, or boisterous with a will of her own? What if they didn't get on? She was plagued by fears. Worst of all, what if Connie didn't like her and that magical chemistry just didn't happen?

Jenny concentrated on deciphering the signposts through the mist and rain. How had she got here, to this moment, on her way to see a Hearing Dog who might, just might, one day be hers? That was as far as she would allow herself to hope. After all, she told herself sternly, life was full of disappointments. No point in getting too excited. Yet up until a few weeks ago the thought that she would ever get a chance to have a Hearing Dog at all had seemed wildly impossible. Her family had thought her mad even to apply. And here she was! Whatever happened now, she had got this far. And ahead of her, on the far side of the floods and rain, just a few miles away, was Connie. Connie, who had the ability, just by loving her back, just by being there, just by 'being her ears', to transform Jenny's life. A warmth stole over her as she thought about Connie. She knew she would love her . . . From the moment she had seen that photograph, she had known.

At last the gates of the Hearing Dog Centre loomed out of the rain. She drove into the rain-washed car park. One way or another—there was no getting away from it—the next few hours would change her life for ever.

Sitting in the reception area at Lewknor, Jenny was a bag of nerves. She could hardly stop her knees shaking. The door opened and Claire Guest came in and introduced herself. There were more forms to fill in. Jenny did everything in a daze. Then she was introduced to Connie's special trainer, Kerry.

'Same name as my daughter,' Jenny smiled. 'That's a good omen!' They both smiled back, responding to Jenny's warmth as so many people did. Connie would like her at once. They could see that.

Jenny balanced a welcome cup of tea on her knee and tried to calm down, struggling to fill in yet more forms without spilling any tea. She had got soaked just getting out of the car, but she hadn't even noticed till now how wet she was. The office was warm and the tea hot. She felt herself thawing out a bit. Outside, the rain lashed against the steamy window, but inside all was tranquillity. Office staff moved about purposefully. An ordinary day. Yet not for her. Did they all know that today Jenny would see her Hearing Dog for the first time? That this was a momentous day for her? Or was it just routine for them? They all seemed to care so much. And after all, that was why they were here, wasn't it? Because of people like her ... because someone, somewhere, had cared enough. The thought made her feel better.

Still there was no sign of Connie. She longed to ask if she could see her. It had been such a long time and she had had such high hopes. She was out there somewhere in those rain-washed grounds, waiting for her. Did she know that Jenny was here?

Claire smiled at her, seeming to understand.

'I'm sorry about all this formality, Jenny. You must be sick of filling in forms. I'm sure you just want to see Connie now, don't you?'

Jenny nodded, close to tears.

'Well, Kerry will go off and get her now. She's in her kennel. It will take a few minutes. Then you can have her for the rest of the day.'

Jenny smiled her thanks. For the rest of the day! She could hardly believe it. She sipped her tea and waited. Hours seemed to pass. Maybe they had forgotten her. Jenny looked at her watch, astonished to see that only a few minutes had gone by after all. Her stomach was rumbling: it had been a long time since breakfast. She had left Davina's house very early, determined not to be late. A good thing, considering the floods she had come through to get here.

The door opened and a black nose appeared, followed by a pair of enquiring brown eyes and two fronded black ears. A black and gold body with a plume of a tail, just like the photograph, yet oh! so different. The real Connie, here, after all the dreaming. Jenny felt her chest tighten with love. She was utterly perfect.

Connie turned back questioningly to her trainer, as though to ask if it was all right, and, sitting down meekly at Kerry's feet as though she belonged to her, she looked at Jenny from across the room. Jenny felt a little pang of jealousy which she instantly suppressed, ashamed of herself. Of course Connie would relate to Kerry. She was her trainer after all, and the most important person in her life at this moment. It would be illogical to expect Connie to love her, Jenny, straight away. It would take time. She mustn't be impatient. All these thoughts passed through Jenny's head in a few seconds. Then, tentatively, she reached out her hand . . .

'Here, Connie. Come here, girl!'

Shy yet questioning, Connie got to her feet in response to a command from Kerry. She came quietly up to Jenny, all the time looking into her face as though searching for something. Whatever it was she saw there must have been just right, for suddenly that beautiful plumed tail began to wag enthusiastically. She pulled forward on her lead, those brown eyes never leaving Jenny's own. Very gently she put her paws on Jenny's lap and lifted her muzzle. Jenny thought her heart would burst. With a shaking hand she stroked the soft, silky fur. A pink tongue emerged and gave her fingers a gentle lick. It was like a message from another world. Here at last was a fellow creature who

92

would share her world, a warm, loving presence in place of isolation. In that moment there was pure understanding. Jenny felt tears spring in her eyes. After all those years of feeling so alone, it was like a miracle . . .

'Oh, I fell in love with her there and then and I knew she was just what I wanted and needed.'

Connie's tail was wagging so hard it seemed as though she would overbalance. She turned her head and tugged the lead from Kerry's hand with her mouth, putting her paws back up on Jenny's lap, the lead dangling comically from her muzzle. Kerry and Jenny both burst out laughing.

'I think she's trying to tell you something,' Kerry signed to Jenny with a smile.

Once again those gentle brown eyes looked deep into Jenny's own, establishing that special telepathy which, in future years, was to be a bond between them.

'Come on!' Connie seemed to be saying. 'Let's get on with it. We've got the rest of our lives together, starting with a walk! I know you love walkies too. There's no time to lose!'

'I expect you could do with some food.' Kerry was smiling at her. 'We don't really have the facilities here, but why don't you walk her down the road for lunch? It's just out of the gate, and turn left. You can't miss the pub. It's about half a mile down the main road.' As though walking your very own Hearing Dog down the road to a pub was an everyday occurrence!

It had stopped raining and the sky had cleared. The sun was shining out of a clear blue sky. A soft wind ruffled the shining puddles. Everything was bright. Diamond drops shimmered on the hawthorn twigs by the gate. The wet road gleamed in the sun. Gold-edged clouds glowed on the horizon. Connie trotted beside Jenny, her tail lifting in the wind, each paw perfectly pointed like a ballerina. She was lovely, the sharp light catching the gold flecks in her coat and the black sheen of her fur, the whole wonderful picture set off by a bright yellow coat. Jenny's heart was full.

She ate her meal in a glow of happiness, hardly tasting a thing. Connie would not get her full Hearing Dog coat and lead until she was fully qualified, but Jenny noticed the difference in the pub immediately she walked in. The red letters on the novice coat, HEARING DOG IN TRAINING, drew interest from everyone. She could almost feel the warmth flowing towards them both. Perhaps it was because the staff were used to Hearing Dogs being 'up the road', and knew a bit about them. They must have seen so many very new owners with very new Hearing Dogs, the handler (if not the dog!) with a dazed expression on her face.

Still, it was so different from walking 'cold' into a new, often intimidating, environment and almost having to do battle to be heard or even treated as a human being. There was somehow no need to break the ice or explain. As soon as Jenny had asked if she could bring Connie in and had told them at the bar (because she was bursting to tell someone!) that she, Jenny, was, she hoped, the new owner, everyone melted into smiles. The staff came up to her and made a fuss of Connie and spoke to Jenny too, looking straight at her so that she could lip-read them quite clearly. It was so different from the normal awkwardness, when she had to explain everything and people seemed to back away rather than take the trouble to make themselves understood.

Maybe she was different, too. She certainly felt different. In those first moments, sitting proudly at a table with Connie at her feet, she felt her confidence begin to grow. Between them they could face anything, go anywhere, do anything!

After being well and truly spoiled by the pub staff (enough to turn any dog's head), Connie had settled quietly under the table, her paws on Jenny's foot. She might have been little more than a puppy, but her behaviour was exemplary: that early training had obviously paid off. And every once in a while she would put her head on Jenny's knee. Jenny could feel the warmth of her breath through her trouser leg. An extraordinary feeling of comfort stole over her. Yes, they were together now. A team. Together they could get through anything that life might throw at them.

Walking back down the road to the Centre in the late afternoon, early dusk already stealing over the sky, Jenny began to dream, for the first time, about what she might do with the rest of her life. It was as though, in those few moments, she had glimpsed something new, a door opening onto a bright new world of possibilities. With Connie beside her the world really was her oyster, here before her, opening up in all its beauty and promise. There would be no stopping them now.

Suddenly, there beside the busy road, cars scudding past, she stopped for a second and stroked that silky coat. Connie's tail wagged furiously and she looked up into Jenny's eyes as she licked her hand. Then it was back on duty as she walked back proudly with Jenny beside her. Jenny could have shouted for joy. For the first time in her life she felt truly and utterly alive.

Stopping at the gate she squatted down beside Connie, holding her head in her hands. Once more, brown eyes looked into brown eyes. Connie licked her on the nose this time and wagged her whole body enthusiastically.

'You've got to go away for a while now, Connie,' Jenny said softly, 'to finish your training. You know that.' With her hands she felt Connie whining softly in her throat, the vibration running right through her body. 'You must do what Kerry tells you. She'll look after you. But then we'll be together. It'll be the beginning for both of us. March 1st—I can't wait!'

Ten

Connie and her sister are both shining examples of dog-hood—loving, brilliantly trained, highly intelligent and utterly dedicated to their particular owners who love them to distraction. However, it must be said that Connie's sister Caldey is free of a few of the little idiosyncrasies that have created Connie's character. In fact Caldey is definitely the good child of the two, although Jenny would never swap Connie for the world. Jenny jokes that Connie never said her prayers, or she would have got Caldey's owner instead; certainly Caldey has a more tranquil existence for a Hearing Dog, although also challenging and full of interest, with new people to get to know. For Caldey's owner, Sister Denise, is a nun, a 'Sister of Charity', not in an enclosed order but living and working in the community. It seems as though a divine chuckle might have been behind the happenstance of one sister going to a nun and the other to a publican . . .

Connie and Caldey grew up looking almost like identical twins, although they had their own separate training programmes and were 'socialised' separately. Caldey, as we know, began her training at the Hearing Dog Centre under the name of Goldie. For a dog who was almost black, despite having more gold flecks in her coat than her sister, the name seemed rather inappropriate. The Centre dictates sensibly that a dog's name, such a vital part of training and of verbal signals, belongs to the dog for life, but as a special case they had agreed to change her name to one which sounded almost exactly the same. Caldey was named after a monastic island off the coast of

Sister Denise (right) and Sister Kathleen with Caldey in the garden of the Marian House, Cardiff. *Photo: Sister Denise*

Caldey touches and tells. 'What is it, Caldey?' *Photo: Sister Denise*

Uldale and The Snooty Fox – a new life for the Harmers and Connie.
Photo: Jenny Harmer

Walking with Jenny by Bassenthwaite Lake. *Photo: Angela Locke*

An ecstatic roll on the grass – Connie's idea of heaven, especially if she can roll in something smelly. *Photo: Jenny Harmer*

She is fascinated by the sea and loves chasing waves. *Photo: Jenny Harmer*

Smokey and Herbie at home among the snooty foxes. Connie's sworn enemies, they have now achieved an uneasy truce. *Photo: Jenny Harmer*

A return visit to Lewknor. Connie hates travelling in cars. She pushed herself through the dog guard and insisted on sitting on the back seat. *Photo: Angela Locke*

Jenny and her friend Davina with Connie.
Photo: Angela Locke

Back at Lewknor, Gillian Lacey shows Connie her new baby. Connie wants to play!
Photo: Angela Locke

Angela meets Connie's trainer, Kerry. Connie would much prefer to go walkies. *Photo: Angela Locke*

Connie and Jenny walking the Cumbria Way. *Photo: Kerry Harmer*

Connie crossing a beck on the Cumbria Way. *Photo: Jenny Harmer*

Jenny and her son Adrian behind the bar of The Snooty Fox. *Photo: Angela Locke*

Geoff, Jenny and some of their Uldale neighbours who are sponsoring a Hearing Dog.
Photo: Jenny Harmer

Sheep on the fells above Uldale. *Photo: Angela Locke*

Wales which had particular significance for Caldey's future owner. She was matched with Caldey after a curious coincidence in which Connie had played an unwitting part. In the summer, when she was still assigned to her socialiser, Connie had returned to the kennels for a brief period, while Caldey was still staying with her own socialiser away from Lewknor. Sister Denise explains:

'Once I knew I had been approved as a possible recipient, the excitement began to mount. Not a day passed when I did not dream about what life would be like once my dog was with me. Summer arrived, and with it an invitation to the Annual Open Day at Lewknor. I drove there full of eagerness. There were lots of fun events, doggie competitions, sideshows, stalls of various kinds . . . in a word, lots to entertain the visitor. But nothing held my attention. There was only one place I wanted to be— and that was in the kennels.

'There were several dogs there, some awaiting assessment, I think, and others at various stages in their training. There were big ones and small, quiet ones and lively ones, mongrels and crosses, and perhaps an occasional pedigree, too. All of them were lovely, dear creatures longing to be with human kind. I liked them all, in that dogs never fail to delight me. But on that occasion I was definitely aware of preferences. I couldn't help asking myself the question: 'If one of these dogs were to be assigned to me, which one would I hope for?' And the answer was clear. It was a lovely Collie cross named Connie. Oh yes! I would love one like that Connie!

'I knew my name was on the waiting list, but had no idea how near the top I might be. I returned home and dreamed. Summer soon gave way to autumn and then autumn relented to the cold, nagging approach of winter. One day in December the long-awaited letter arrived, inviting me to come to Lewknor to meet the dog which was proposed for me. The enclosed photo showed a beautiful Collie x Retriever bitch. I was over the moon.

'December 21st found me at the Training Centre to meet my future companion and assistant. What a beauty she was! And what a character! Yes, she would be fine for me. It was love at first sight.'

Strange that the recipients of both dogs should use the same heartfelt phrase when they saw their dogs for the first time.

Denise continues:

'Home again and more waiting. Come March '93 I was back in Lewknor—this time for a residential training course with my dog. One day at breaktime I was chatting to Andy, one of the trainers. He said to me: "Did you know that your Hearing Dog has a sister, also trained here?" It was the first I'd heard of it, and I was really interested. "She finished a few weeks ago," he said. "Her name is Connie."

'I was flabbergasted! My wish had come true. I could hardly have got a dog more like Connie than that!'

When Sister Denise and Jenny met for the first time, as a result of this book, they found they had a lot in common and got on famously. In fact both of them, in their way, are doing similar kind of work now that Jenny has become actively involved in the Deaf community—on top of being a very busy publican.

It all began with my fax machine springing into life at 11 o'clock at night—pages and pages of beautifully-typed material, accompanied by some witty cartoons at the side of the script. This was my first intriguing contact with Sister Denise. I had thought it would be very interesting to make contact with her and had sent a letter to Hearing Dogs for the Deaf, which Gillian Lacey had kindly agreed to forward. I felt it was rather like sending a letter into outer space and not being sure where it would land. Yet here it was—the response. I had just got out of the bath, but stood riveted reading the pages upside down and laughing at the cartoons. Wonderful humour sprang off the pages as I read them.

I don't know why I had imagined that a nun would be anything different; I suppose my knowledge of nuns was rather limited. Delightfully, that was about to change. A few days later, when I was working at my desk, I had a phone call. A soft Irish voice spoke at the other end, and then I quickly understood that my answers were being 'translated' by a hearing person in the background. We got in a bit of a muddle at first and I kept interrupting, not used to trying to listen and then respond, but we had a long and fascinating conversation, the first of several. More weeks passed and then once again I heard that soft Irish lilt on the phone. Denise and her friend Kathleen had decided to come to Keswick, where Kathleen had family connections. They were going to stay in a guest-house and would like to meet up with me, and also meet Jenny. I was thrilled and we arranged for them to visit me at home, here in the Lake District. Just before they all arrived, and too late to bake a cake, I realised that the very day we had agreed, December 6th, was also Connie's and Caldey's fifth birthday. It would be a very special day indeed, and a real coincidence, as none of us had realised its significance.

A bright blue van came down the hill driven by a woman with curly grey hair framing a sweet face. I had been expecting nuns in habits but these were in ordinary clothes. Sister Kathleen got out of the passenger side and shook hands with a warm smile. Then out from the back of the van came an almost perfect copy of Connie, except that her ears were longer and more fronded (Jenny keeps Connie's ears trimmed as they tend to get tangled).

We began to walk up the hill. Caldey, just like Connie, was very shy of my excitable labradors who wanted to play, and preferred to stay at Sister Denise's side, looking rather protective and jealous. However, once in the field she began tentatively to relax. It was like watching a re-run of Connie.

It was a beautiful bright, frosty day with snow on the tops. We climbed to the top of the fell and looked out at the beauty of the snow-covered Lake District. There was a shout from down below: Jenny had arrived with Connie. I watched, amazed, as Caldey ran down the hill and greeted her sister. Two fronded tails waved. Immediately they began to run round each other like puppies. My two dogs were quite left out! It was as if the dogs had known each other all their lives. Perhaps littermates always remember each other, yet was I being imaginative in seeing a strong relationship between the two as they rolled over and over in a slow, serious form of play which seemed to suit them both?

We took some photographs against the white fells and talked and laughed. I began to learn a little about the work of these two extraordinary women. Vincent de Paul, who founded the order in France in 1633, during the time of the Civil War, told the Sisters to be ready to go to anyone who needed them—the sick, orphans, soldiers, prisoners, refugees and the aged. This is a vow which the Sisters have kept ever since, working all over the world in a modified form of the traditional habit, with the poor and dispossessed. It had been Sister Denise's task to found a centre for deaf people in Cardiff. Both Sisters work with the profoundly deaf and have a great insight into the needs of the Deaf community.

We spent a lovely day together. My husband cooked lunch for us and we gave the dogs some treats as a celebration for being birthday girls. Jenny and Connie had to dash off to an appointment, but Denise and Kathleen, with Caldey asleep at our feet, sat talking for many hours, until suddenly it was time to go. We said goodbye with much affection. I felt so privileged to have seen a little of these two fascinating women, who explained to me that they were taking a sabbatical from their work, which was why they were not in their normal habits. However, they left me a photograph of themselves in their 'working gear'. Since then we have had much contact and they have become valued friends.

Denise's experience of deafness, as both she and Jenny were anxious to stress when they met, was very different from Jenny's own, and was perhaps more typical of applicants for Hearing Dogs. Most Hearing Dogs actually go to those with acquired deafness, who have not had a lifetime of experience in adapting to the absence of sound and may be floundering to come to terms with practical functions in a world that assumes response to sound as the 'norm'. Jenny, partially deaf since birth, had at least worked out strategies for survival, however limiting and frustrating they might still have been. To manage the normality of life when, sometimes as suddenly as between one morning and the next, a person may be plunged into utter silence, is a different challenge indeed, and one which the provision of Hearing Dogs addresses particularly well.

Jenny points out that she has, after all, always been deaf and had had many years of adjustment from childhood, however traumatic. She had struggled from her earliest years to cope in a world without sound and had at least had a chance to adapt accordingly. Looking back, she feels she was always part of the Deaf world. However much cruelty and insensitivity that had meant in the early years at the Royal School for the Deaf, and however much rejection, there were always others around who were in exactly the same boat, suffering and experiencing the same deprivations.

Yet for many people who become suddenly deaf later in life, the trauma is almost impossible to come to terms with. They have acquired the linguistic skills of many years of hearing, and feel themselves part of the hearing world, yet now are cruelly cut off and helpless. All their friends are hearing, and they have made a life for themselves in a totally hearing environment with no preparation for the abrupt change to a world of silence. Those with acquired deafness speak of 'mourning' for their hearing, and this is a clear indication of the terrible pain of suddenly losing a whole sense. So much learnt over a whole lifetime of hearing experience has to be relearnt and adapted and a new mode of communication, a new lifestyle, adopted.

Experts on deafness make distinctions too between those who think in images, never having had spoken language, and those who have learnt verbal language from childhood and thus use words as the building blocks of thought. Jenny is remarkable in the amount of verbal skill she has, perhaps because she had some residual hearing as a small child. Yet, conversely, only in the last few years has she really been exploring the wonders of sign language which she feels so passionately is her 'own' language, as the Deaf world is her own world.

For Jenny and Denise the practical help with the alarm clocks and cooker timers, doorbells and the like is invaluable, bestowing independence, but Connie and Caldey also mean something much more profound, which has changed both women's lives. Perhaps for every deaf person who acquires a Hearing Dog there is something special, bound to their own life and to their own unique experience, far beyond the practical details of everyday living, however vital those may be. It is that close companionship, that end to isolation. For each and every recipient of a Hearing Dog there will be that special dimension, a unique, life-changing element which is, for each person, his or her own particular miracle.

Eleven

Hearing Dogs for Deaf People always stresses that dogs are on permanent loan to their deaf 'owners'—a safety net in case something goes wrong with the dog's welfare or the deaf handler's situation changes. Such protection for the Hearing Dogs is a vital part of the organisation's philosophy, enabling life-long monitoring and care. However, to all intents and purposes, outside that understanding, Connie was to be assigned to Jenny for life. They were pronounced a perfect match by the team at Lewknor, and now the hard work was to begin.

Kerry and Claire had to consider what Jenny's specific needs would be and fit Connie's training around that, with the environment of a pub particularly in mind. Connie's gentle, submissive nature meant that she was still quite shy with strangers, and there would be a lot of those in a pub. Jenny would be spending a great deal of time in the kitchen, and Connie would have to be used to the often hectic routine of a pub and restaurant. Health regulations dictated that she would not be allowed into the kitchen itself, except for specific sound work, and would have to have a basket just outside the cooking area. Response to the cooker timer would be very important.

Connie would certainly have to be very adaptable. Some of her life might be spent in a quiet, very isolated place such as the cottage at Plas Coch, but at other times she would need to work in an environment which would be very distracting, full of unknown people who could walk in and out of 'home' at will. It was quite a challenge for any dog.

Connie was due to spend almost four more months at the Hearing Dog Centre where her real work would begin with her trainer, Kerry. Only Hearing Dogs are trained at Lewknor, by the Centre's staff, and over the years a highly specialised system of training has been evolved.

Most Hearing Dogs carry out the major part of their work in a home environment, although they are taken to work by some owners. In Jenny's case, for the most part, home and work would be mixed up together. The home environment is the start for all basic training of 'touch and tell', and with this in mind a purpose-built training block, which resembles a real house, has been built at Lewknor. Here are all the things that a dog might expect to find in its own home, each with particular challenges and required responses which would have to be learnt for the animal's future work.

On that first morning of formal training, Kerry encouraged Connie to explore each room in turn, until she was thoroughly familiar with everything around her. After all, she would spend a great deal of concentrated time here in the next few months. Connie ran about, sniffing and investigating, already interested. There was a kitchen and bedroom and lounge, all set out with furniture, and there were lots of doors. Here was a glass door which would help a dog going to a house with a see-through door to be trained for the doorbell, and here too was a wooden door, where the dog would be trained to rely on the sound of the doorbell alone. There was a real kitchen with cookers, and even a smell of real food (sadly not in evidence!). There were windows and chairs which smelled of people. It was all very intriguing.

Connie had been chosen for her interest in and sensitivity to sound when she had her initial assessment. Now that interest began to form an integral part of her training, beginning with a basic reaction to a squeaker toy. The squeaker is the first listening device used for training and consists of a small round piece of rubber about the size of a 50p piece. From this simple device, all else follows. The dogs are trained to touch the person who has the squeaker, and it will always be used in the initial stages when training the dog to a new sound, or later on, if the dog is not responding well to any situation and needs a 'top-up' in training terms.

Kerry, operating in a pair with another trainer, set out to use this basic sound, the squeaker, working on developing Connie's responses. The idea was to build up the vital association in the dog's mind between sound and touch. Gradually Connie would progress to the idea that she must go and touch the handler or owner, alerting her to the sound.

So on that first morning Kerry, the squeaker hidden in her hand behind her back, began to play a game. The squeaker squealed intriguingly, and Connie put her head on one side, listening. There it was again! What could it be, and where was it coming from? Was it a mouse? Connie located the sound: it was definitely coming from Kerry. She was being encouraged to approach her, just like a game. Now she was being encouraged to put up a paw on Kerry's lap.

'Good girl! What a clever girl!'

She had obviously done the right thing. Kerry made a big fuss of her, fondling her soft ears.

'Now, just like this . . .'

Every time she heard the squeaker, Connie was encouraged to put up a paw. This was easy, and the best part was that, every time she did it, she was rewarded with a titbit. The next stage was harder. When she heard the noise, she had to go to the other trainer and tell her. That wasn't quite so simple, but Connie, highly intelligent, was quick to grasp it. And whatever was in those titbits they were delicious, worth playing the game for.

As the weeks passed Connie threw herself into her

training with enthusiasm, showing her extraordinary intelligence and willingness to learn. In that first week the squeaker was gradually replaced by the sound of a wind-up alarm clock—the right sound for Jenny at that time. They had to go upstairs for that, and one of the trainers pretended to be asleep. (Connie knew she wasn't. After all, she still had her clothes on.) Still, it was a lovely game and she would probably get one of those delicious titbits at the end.

The alarm clock went off and, very quickly, she could see what she had to do. There was the sound, and she knew by now she had to tell Kerry. The first few times she got very excited and jumped on the bed, almost crushing Kerry by putting her paws on her chest. That would be all right for a little dog, but not for a dog the size of a Golden Retriever. Gradually, she learned that she had to use her paw, very, very gently. Yes, just like that. What a good dog!

The absolutely vital part of her training would be learning to touch gently in order to alert her owner to the various different sounds. Not every sound—a lorry rumbling past the window or noises on the television weren't on the list—not this list anyway. No, it would be specific sounds she would learn to recognise, which her owner would need to be told about, and this was one of them. Jenny would need to know it was time to get up and this noise was something she had to be alerted to—straight away, however warm and comfortable Connie might be in her basket on a cold winter's morning. And she must be woken gently, not with too much of shock for a sleeping person who would have no idea that an alarm clock had just gone off. A gentle greeting to say, 'It's time to get up!' Much better than those awful flashing lights. Jenny had had quite enough of those.

Then they had to go back down into the little kitchen. This time there was a different sound, a cooker timer beeping away. Kerry wasn't lying down this time, but relaxing in a chair in the sitting-room, reading a magazine. Couldn't she hear that noise? Connie was sure she could, but she seemed to be waiting for Connie to tell her anyway. Suddenly it dawned on Connie. This was like the upstairs game. She had to put her paw up and touch Kerry, as she had before, telling her about the noise. Then she would get a titbit and a big fuss made of her. But she couldn't reach Kerry's cheek from there. What could she do?

Kerry, pretending to be deeply absorbed in her magazine, found it suddenly knocked to the ground as Connie half-landed on her lap in order to put a paw up to her face. No, not like that! Like this!

The cooker timer went off again, and this time Connie came and sat beside Kerry, looking up into her face, before putting one paw firmly on her lap. This time she got a big titbit and lots of loving. Kerry was pleased! Kerry was the centre of her world, and pleasing her was more important than anything.

Later Connie would learn that, when she had got Kerry's attention, she must lead her through to the kitchen. Small dogs were trained to jump up, while medium-sized dogs were taught to sit and put two paws onto their owner's lap. But Connie, who was a big dog, was to be taught to place one paw on her owner's lap or arm to attract attention. Anything more would be rather too much.

It was time for a break and a play outside on the grass, and then a walk in the beautiful grounds. There were several other dogs also undertaking their training at the same time, all destined for different kinds of homes. Big, small, medium, they had a wonderful game together, able to relax for a while. Caldey was there too, waiting to start her own training in a few weeks. They had a lovely romp.

The training continued, day after day. Connie was really getting the hang of it all. As the weeks passed her trainer recorded excellent progress. It was a good game, however serious the purpose, with rewards at the end of each successful 'touch and tell', alerting the trainer to the specific sound. By the second week Kerry was able to write in Connie's file that she was 'getting better all the time. Teaching the dog to lead the person'. By week six Connie was responding to the telephone and doorbell from all over the house as Kerry gradually built up the repertoire of sounds. Connie had become adept at waking her trainer by putting two paws on the bed, while on the command 'Connie fetch Jenny', she would go out and touch and fetch the person playing Jenny. By week 12 Kerry reported in her notes that Connie was confident with this next stage and would readily 'fetch' the person playing Jenny anywhere in the house, upstairs or downstairs.

By week 13 Connie had made such good progress that training began on that vitally important element in a Hearing Dog's sound vocabulary, the smoke/fire alarm. This might be a life-or-death situation for dog and owner. It is rare in shops and other public places to find smoke alarms which do anything but emit an ear-splitting noise. Certainly no flashing lights. No problem for a hearing population, but as Jenny had found to her cost, that day she had emerged from the Ladies at her workplace to find the building deserted, the noise is totally lost on a deaf person. If only Connie had been there on that day, how much less frightening it would have been. Very, very few public places, and most of those of a specialist nature, have a flashing light to accompany the alarm. So one of the Hearing Dog's most vital tasks is to give a clear, unequivocal indication that a fire alarm has just gone off, an indication which could not possibly be confused with any other signal to the owner. Once the Hearing Dog hears a smoke/fire alarm, it must immediately lie down at the owner's feet.

This signal, still touching the owner to convey the normal sound response, but lying down instead of leading her to the source of the sound, which could be leading her into danger, is then translated into any situation where the owner may be in peril. This is where the dog's intelligence comes into play. Connie, for example, will not react, other than with normal caution, to everyday traffic in a town, but on several occasions has stopped in her tracks on a narrow country lane and looked back at Jenny to tell her that there is traffic coming towards them.

Sister Denise owes her life to Caldey's response to danger, for she once lay down in front of her to stop her using a pedestrian crossing, even though the 'green man' was showing clearly. Seconds later an ambulance, sirens blaring, came racing round the corner and straight through the red light, right across the middle of the crossing.

By week 14 Kerry reported that she had gone to give a talk about the work of the Hearing Dog Centre, that Connie had gone with her and that she was very good indeed. Weeks 16 and 17 went past with more glowing reports. Connie was making excellent progress in her training and had acquired all the skills necessary for a fully trained Hearing Dog. It was time to meet Jenny again, to spend a week getting to know her properly, and for the vital work of 'bedding down' the two of them together so that they became a unique, fully-functioning team. This would be the crunch point for them both. If they didn't 'jell' together now, even after all the encouraging signs from their first meeting, if Connie couldn't respond to Jenny and Jenny wasn't right for her, it would almost be back to square one for each of them, although nothing could take away Connie's basic training. That would be there now, for life.

It would be a hard challenge for them both—for Jenny, for whom all this would be a totally new experience, working with her own Hearing Dog, and for Connie who had grown to love her trainer Kerry, related so closely to her and did everything to please her. Kerry had always been careful to make sure that Connie worked with other trainers, so that she didn't get too fond of just her alone— but Connie was a very affectionate dog. Would Jenny be able to take Kerry's place in her devotion and, even more, become Connie's beloved person? Would Jenny and Connie be able to bond for life?

It was time for week 18 . . .

Twelve

Most of the first week that dog and future owner spend together at Lewknor is about training the owner. The dog, after all, has already undergone rigorous training, only needing to transfer this onto another human being. This vital week in the flat is designed to teach the new handler/ owner to look after the dog to the highest standards, to cope with going into town for shopping and to meet all the challenges of normal life. Very importantly, the owner will be taught what she should expect of the dog's responses in every situation.

Jenny tried to reassure herself as she drove down the still wintry roads to stay with Davina. Hadn't they got on really well to start with, she and Connie? True, Connie was still obviously 'bonded' to Kerry and her other trainers, but when they had gone off for their walk down to the pub that day it had been wonderful, as though they had always been together. Connie had seemed quite at home with Jenny. It had been a good beginning, hadn't it?

Jenny was due at Lewknor the next morning, to begin her week's training process with Connie. She left Davina's early. Despite it being the beginning of March the sky looked threatening, and as she travelled up to Lewknor there was more snow. Jenny thought back to her last trip, when she had met Connie for the first time. Then there had been floods, and she had wondered if she was going to get through to the Centre.

She arrived safely in good time, yet full of nerves once again. This time, however, there were familiar, welcoming faces around her and it didn't seem so intimidating. She was given a cup of hot coffee; the atmosphere was supportive and kind. Jenny began to feel better. The door opened and Connie came in, without her training coat, looking sleek and beautiful. She had obviously just been bathed in honour of the occasion.

Kerry gave her a reassuring smile and Connie, looking up at Kerry, making sure it was all right, came tentatively forward just as she had the last time, gently putting her wet nose into Jenny's hand. Jenny's heart turned over with love, although she had to suppress a twinge of jealousy that once again Connie related so much to Kerry and not to her. Would a week be long enough to change that?

Kerry took Jenny and Connie outside and showed them the flat where they would be staying: a purpose-built, one-storey building with all the facilities they would need for training. It seemed comfortable and warm. Then Kerry left them to it.

'I'll be back this afternoon and we'll go through some training, but it's time for you to get to know each other!'

The door shut behind her. Connie and Jenny were alone in the flat. Jenny sat down in an armchair and held out her hand to Connie. Shyly, Connie came forward and placed her fine-boned head on Jenny's lap. Oh, she was so beautiful! Connie looked up at Jenny with intelligent brown eyes. Once again, as before, something profound passed between them. Jenny felt her heart spill over with emotion. She stroked the soft head and the silky ears with those distinctive golden-black strands of fine hair. Yes, she was just perfect. The most perfect dog in the world. What had she, Jenny, done to deserve a dog like this?

'You are just beautiful. You know that? And I'm going to look after you so well. We are going to get on together brilliantly. We'll have walkies together, and play together, and you'll meet Geoff and Kerry and Adrian and the cats

. . . oh, I do hope the cats will be all right. We'll have to see about that.'

She spoke softly, looking into Connie's eyes. Connie's fronded tail banged on the carpet. She seemed to be taking in every word.

That first afternoon was spent getting used to Connie and training her alongside Kerry, patiently rehearsing the same procedures that Kerry and the other trainers had gone through so thoroughly in the preceding months. Soon it would not be a rehearsal. Soon, Jenny would be depending on Connie for real.

By the end of the day Jenny was exhausted. Who would have thought that it would all be so intensive? She was so looking forward to getting to bed and having the flat to herself, just with Connie lying in her basket beside her. Time together, time to get to know one another . . . She was quite upset to hear that another girl was staying with her that night, a candidate for a Hearing Dog who had an interview the next day. The other girl didn't arrive until almost midnight. Jenny fell into bed, absolutely worn out with the emotional and physical demands of the day.

Connie was curled up in her basket, her deep brown eyes watching Jenny as she climbed into bed. She must wonder why she isn't in her kennel, Jenny thought. It must all seem so strange to her.

'Don't forget to wake me, Connie,' Jennie said drowsily before her head touched the pillow. She was instantly asleep.

The next morning she woke suddenly and heavily and looked at the alarm clock. It was 7.40. She was late! Connie had obviously ignored the alarm completely and was still asleep in her basket. It must have run merrily until the mechanism had stopped.

Jenny roused Connie, who seemed slow and tired. Perhaps she too was exhausted with all these bewildering new challenges. But what should Jenny do? She found herself starting the day with a headache and all upside down. It was not a good beginning. Would it ever be right? She told Kerry about Connie's failure to respond to the alarm, feeling somehow quite traitorous. Kerry was at pains to allay her worries and explained how she should respond if it happened the next morning. This was quite common, Kerry assured her, and she wasn't to get too concerned, otherwise her worries would communicate themselves to Connie and it would be much harder for them both.

They had a very active day doing obedience and sound work in the morning and going into town for the afternoon. Kerry took another dog who was at the end of training. It was quite hectic controlling the animals and doing the shopping too. Jenny was relieved when the two of them were again left together. There was no one else in the flat, thank goodness, and she managed to get an early night. Connie went straight to her basket by Jenny's bed while Jenny read for a little while, trying to unwind. Then, before going to sleep, she got up and gave Connie a stroke, showing her the alarm clock as she wound it up and checked the time.

'Don't forget the alarm in the morning, Connie, will you?'

Connie banged her tail. Jenny stroked her soft head. 'I am relying on you.'

The next morning, after a good night's sleep, Jenny woke before the alarm. She lay in bed watching the minute hand of the clock move round, wondering how Connie would react. The moment came when Jenny knew the alarm clock must be ringing. Connie opened one eye . . . and went back to sleep.

This was never going to work! Remembering Kerry's advice, and while the alarm was, she hoped, still ringing, she called to Connie, encouraging her to come over to the bed and put her paws up as she had been taught.

'Come on, Connie. Good girl!'

Hearing her name, Connie opened her eyes again with a long-suffering expression. Despite her despair, that look almost made Jenny burst out laughing, it was so comical. Slowly, with every appearance of martyrdom, Connie sat up and stretched laboriously. Then, at last, she came waddling over to Jenny's side of the bed, put her paws up on the bed and touched Jenny's cheek. Well, it wasn't exactly according to the book, but it was a big step forward. Jenny praised Connie extravagantly and gave her a titbit from the bedside table. She felt they had overcome a huge obstacle. Tomorrow would be even better.

When I shared a room with Jenny on our trip to Lewknor, I had been particularly looking forward to seeing Connie going through her alarm call routine and hoped to capture the moment on camera. I awoke early and lay watching the clock, waiting for the alarm to go off. Jenny, exhausted after the long journey of the previous day, was fast asleep on her tummy.

The moment came at last and I was ready with my camera. The alarm made a terrific racket, but Connie, using her extraordinary intelligence, had worked out that, since I could hear, she could leave the job to me. As the alarm continued to make its terrible noise she came round to me, looking expectant. I could feel her eyes boring into me. She was quite obviously hoping that I would be the one to wake her mistress. I lay there with my eyes half-closed, waiting to see what she would do. She went back and looked at Jenny. My camera, primed with a flash, was ready for action. Oh, no! Connie was coming round to me again with a questioning look in her eyes. I had really let her down now! She definitely thought that it was my job to wake Jenny. Why should she do it? Maybe she saw how tired Jenny was, and didn't want to be the one to disturb her. Much better coming from me.

Eventually, with an audible sigh of disappointment, which spoke volumes, Connie made her way round the end of Jenny's bed and gently licked her mistress's hand where it lay on the pillow. Then, casting a reproachful glance at me, she put her two front paws on the bed and softly, with one paw raised, touched Jenny's half-visible cheek with her pad. Success at last. The trouble was that I was struggling with the flash which had given up the ghost in the dim light, and I didn't get my picture!

At Lewknor on that second morning the training went well, with Jenny learning how to groom Connie and all the veterinary information that she would need to look after her as well as possible. In the evening she started up the car, thinking she would take Connie for a run. It was a bit of a tussle getting her in the back, and she cowered in the far corner, while Jenny tried to reassure her. She appeared terrified. It was a real setback. Jenny wondered how on earth she was going to cope with the trip home. With the help of titbits scattered in the car and a lot of love, talking to Connie to calm her down, they eventually made what seemed like a very long trip indeed, to the garage up the road to get some oil. She must talk to Kerry again. Yet another problem to worry about. It was not going to be easy.

On the third morning, Jenny was genuinely asleep when suddenly she felt the gentlest touch of a paw on her face. Opening her eyes she saw in front of her the dim silhouette of Connie, looking down at her, one paw raised. Connie, behaving as though she had been doing this all her life! She had responded perfectly to the alarm. It was like a miracle. Pleased with herself, she gave Jenny a huge wet lick. She knew she had done well!

'Thanks, Connie, I know I haven't washed yet today. Give me a chance!' It was a wonderful moment. Jenny felt on top of the world.

From then on it was as though Connie had suddenly realised that Jenny was to be her 'Kerry'—for ever—and she was going to be Connie's special responsibility. Kerry reported in her notes that Connie was already very good in the flat, even though there had been a few teething troubles with the alarm clock. One of the most crucial things was that Connie and Jenny were building up a very good relationship. Despite Jenny's early fears, Kerry, with all her experience, could see from the outside how close these two were destined to become. Already, when Jenny was out of the room for a few moments, Connie would watch the door, waiting for her new mistress to come back. Teething troubles there might be, but that relationship was there, growing in strength all the time. Kerry had done her job magnificently, and that magical chemistry between Jenny and Connie, impossible to predict or plan for, was beginning to 'fizz'.

They grew closer and closer during that week, going for walks together, which they both loved, whenever they could get away from training. Jenny found that Connie behaved very well off the lead, responding and coming back when she was called. On the last evening Davina arrived and they went out for a meal together, a rather dispiriting experience as Jenny found there was nowhere nearby that would accept a Hearing Dog in the restaurant. There were obviously more battles to be fought, even this near to the Lewknor Centre. Eventually they found a place where they were reluctantly allowed in, but it was an awful meal. Yet having Connie beside her made it a special occasion nonetheless. Jenny was full of pride, looking at Connie sitting there, as good as gold in her training coat. And everyone made such a fuss of her. So much had been achieved. She felt as though she and Connie had always been together . . .

'The week at Oxford had passed very quickly, and it was all as if I was sleepwalking and soon I would wake and find it was a dream. I was very gentle with Connie and I was petrified of hurting her. She oozed such sweetness that I'd melt under her gaze. It was impossible for me to raise my voice at her. There was, however, little need for that as she was so eager to please . . .

'There was only one startling discovery at that time— Connie's fear of the car. She'd go all tensed up and continue so until the journey's end, however long it took. When I first discovered this I went off, in a panic, to Kerry, and was advised to feed her in the boot of our estate car to try to get her accustomed to it. To this day she still hates going in the car and took to hiding anywhere when she heard my keys.'

Although Kerry and Jenny had spent a lot of time that week working on the problem of the car, and Connie was certainly getting better, secretly Jenny was dreading the journey home. After a final session of sound and obedience work, they were to set off at lunchtime for Wales.

'It was time to face the journey. Golly, she was so precious, I might just as well have had a large piece of Delft pottery in the car. Corners had to be negotiated with great care in case I added to the stress of the experience. It was a long journey and I took many stops, and each time feared I might not get her to go back into the car. The thought of using the radio hadn't entered my head, as being deaf this piece of equipment is incomprehensible, so I talked and sang to her all the way. I'll never know if this kept her spirits up but it certainly made my voice hoarse.'

At last familiar signposts came into view. Not long now . . . Connie, seeming to sense that her new home was near, sat up in the dark. Jenny could see her dimly illuminated against the occasional street-light in the rear-view mirror, before they were once again driving through the darkness of the remote Welsh countryside, and she could see nothing in the mirror.

They turned into the little lane that led to home. They had made it! She was coming home with Connie, and nothing would ever be the same again. Those five days at

Lewknor had changed her life for ever, she knew it. It was the beginning of a whole new existence, full of promise for them both.

Her throat was sore with singing for the last few miles, but Jenny grinned to herself. Even with her singing voice (which was supposed not to be too bad, though she had no way of knowing), Connie was probably putting her paws over her ears. Her throat was rasping after all those hours of free entertainment. God knows what she had sounded like towards the end!

She spoke once more into the darkness, a surge of happiness washing over her:

'We're nearly there, Connie! You'll love it, I promise. You wait till you see the sea, and the mountains! This will be your home, only for a few weeks, but we'll make the most of it, won't we? Then we'll be moving to somewhere even more wonderful. We're going to move to the Lake District. Walkies in the mountains. Won't it be wonderful! You and I together . . . for always.'

The lights were on in the cottage at the end of the lane. They would all be waiting for her, her whole family turning out to see the new family member.

'I want us to be best friends. I need you, Connie. I need you to be my ears. I've needed you for a long time, so I can get on with my life, and I want to give you a wonderful life too . . . This is just the beginning.'

PART 3

A Whole New World Beyond

Thirteen

'Perfect, absolutely perfect! I got to thinking they had made a superb match, and I felt overwhelmed and very grateful that they had given me such a dog. My heart was truly full. And even today, when she walks ahead of me, this feeling returns. It's a very special kind of love and it signifies my deep regard for all she does for me, all that she does without asking for anything in return. We have built up such a good rapport and understanding of one another that I always seem to know when it is time to let her go about her business. She knows my moods and feelings and never allows me to feel low; she comes up and puts her cold nose in my hand, and I am immediately transformed. I have such intense love for her and my heart wells up. It is a different kind of love, not like the human kind, but so very special in its own way.

'Once home, it was "showing off" time. Many people remember the beautiful black dog who became all stiff in a car! She explored the house and seemed baffled by all the nooks and crannies. She wasn't very keen on the stairs as they were open-plan and a little slippy.'

Connie, with her shy, gentle ways, was an instant hit with the family, and she seemed to feel at home with them immediately. But there would be little enough time for the two of them to relax and get to know each other and for Connie to find out about this new place, for they were due to move to the Lake District in a month's time. Just a month for Connie to settle in and everything would begin again. In those first days Jenny found that all she wanted to do was to walk alone with Connie, to build up that precious relationship, and for them to get to know one another. Their walks together became a wonderful resource, a time when they could both find peace and quiet away from the stresses of an increasingly busy life; a time of solitude and yet companionship which was to be part of their unique partnership. And Connie so loved being outdoors that it made their walks a joy.

'I knew she loved the countryside, and I have always felt that this is one little way I can repay her for all she does. We went to all the old haunts I used to visit with Blue, but now it was really special because I had such a helper too. Right from the start Connie skipped and rolled around in the fields when she had her freedom, her pleasure was so obvious . . .'

Her walks were what she truly lived for. Jenny could see that Connie felt here, in the countryside, running free, that she was not on duty and was really able to relax.

As she had promised, Jenny took Connie down to the sea at Aberdovey. It was the first time that the dog had seen the sea and she went quite mad. Jenny couldn't help laughing at her as she chased the waves backwards and forwards, running madly up the beach as though she was afraid they would swallow her up. As she watched, Jenny was reminded that in many ways Connie was still a puppy at heart, despite her serious responsibilities. It was important for her to have time to play—after all, she had to work very hard.

After only eight days together, Jenny noted in her diary that Connie seemed to be doing very well, considering everything was so strange. On the morning of 9 March Gillian Lacey, the Placement Officer and co-founder of Hearing Dogs, arrived. Connie and Jenny spent the whole day working with her, although there was still time for a romp in the field with Gillian's dog Gemma. Gillian stayed for a day and a night, and Jenny really enjoyed having her there and welcomed her sympathetic support.

Together they visited the vet in Aberdovey, who gave Connie a thorough examination, pronouncing her very fit. Jenny found herself swelling with pride.

Those first few precious weeks in Wales were a lovely time, with less work to be done as they were packing up to leave for the Lake District. Connie had at last got the hang of the alarm clock (although Jenny eventually changed it for an electronic one). Getting to know Connie, and becoming part of the relationship with her, was a truly wonderful experience. They had lots of magical walks around the Welsh countryside, enjoying the early spring, and there were plenty of chances to go to the sea so that Connie could play her special game of chasing the waves.

There were a few little hiccups in the beginning. One potential problem, which Jenny had not really anticipated, was the two cats Herbie and Smokey. From the moment they saw Connie there began a war of attrition which has carried on to this day. Sadly, it was Connie who was to blame. She immediately took it into her head to chase Herbie whenever she saw him, although mysteriously ignoring Smokey. Nowadays the two seem to have reached an uneasy truce, but one is never quite sure how long it will last.

Another problem was that the cottage in Wales was quite isolated, and few of Jenny's friends came to call. It was difficult for Connie to get in much practice with the doorbell from people arriving unexpectedly. Later, when they moved to Cumbria, to The Snooty Fox, everyone just walked in without ringing the bell. From the beginning they kept open house there, and those first weeks in Wales, when there were so few people to practise on, made it much harder for Connie to adjust to this.

There were hilarious moments too. The stairs at Plas Coch had not been quite finished in the renovation and, worse still, were narrow and went round in a curve. Connie found them very challenging and several times nearly lost her footing, sliding round the curve with her paws flat, looking most apprehensive. Eventually she gave up and refused to attempt them, so it was just as well they were moving.

The Snooty Fox was due to open in April and they had only one week to get ready once they moved in. This beautiful inn had been empty when they took it over and the goodwill would need building up. It was nevertheless in a prime area on the edge of the Lake District, and April was one of the most popular times for tourists. Springtime, and its associations with Wordsworth's daffodils, snow on the tops, blossom-time and new-born lambs, lure thousands of people every year into this most beautiful part of England.

Jenny remembers those weeks as a complete daze. Not only was she adjusting to the whole concept of running her own business as an equal partner, but at the same time she was trying to get used to a Hearing Dog, while Connie was trying to get used to her. Despite the pressures of work, this was still a time of training, an absolutely vital period. Jenny had to discipline herself to practise sound work and generally help Connie to settle.

The positive side of moving from the cottage in Wales was that Jenny sensed immediately that Connie loved Cumbria. There was something about her demeanour and a sort of extra spring in her step. Jenny was already beginning to 'read' Connie and her moods. Perhaps it was something to do with having a Collie for a mother, for she had certainly loved Wales, and a hill life was obviously in her blood. It was just that Cumbria seemed the right place for her, even more than the hills and the sea of Wales. It made Jenny feel better about the rushed move, which was hardly an ideal start for a Hearing Dog. Once on the fellside Connie seemed to jump for joy, running here and there in the grass, always ending up with a good roll which often resulted in a smelly coat and a grin from ear to ear. She must have known that this would mean one of those detestable baths, but the pleasure seemed worth it.

During those first crucial weeks Connie and Jenny were being overseen by the Centre at Lewknor, getting every assistance as well as visits to ensure that all was well with dog and owner. Throughout that time they were working to get ready for an important day, 17 June, when Connie would take her final test. The Snooty Fox had opened in April as planned and immediately began to trade successfully, an indication of the popularity they would build on in the future. The lovely little pub, half-hidden in its secret valley, very quickly became a magnet for walkers and holidaymakers, a trend that continues to this day. But sometimes the local people and visitors were faced with a surprising sight.

'Connie wasn't a fully trained Hearing Dog as yet, so we had to practise very hard to ensure she worked as well in the home as she had at the Centre. This meant that family members had to help out, either by going outside and ringing the doorbell or by trudging off to the nearest telephone box to phone home.

'The sight of Geoff ringing his own doorbell brought looks of amazement to the faces of passers-by, especially if they were known to us. And calling from a phone box when it was known we had a telephone kept up all the suspense.

'Then there was the fire alarm, an important part of the practice procedures but hated by all. The noise was quite something, so I am told, and to see Geoff appear after the practice, seemingly with his head whirling, made me realise how loud it must be to him. Always this practice was done before opening times, and it often brought people to their windows wondering if everything was all right at the pub.'

While they had been in Wales, many people who caught

sight of Connie, that beautiful black dog with the yellow coat, were intrigued and interested. But the situation there was much more isolated. Here in the Lake District she attracted considerable attention from the beginning, especially as she was the first Hearing Dog in Cumbria.

Connie had her work cut out, meeting all the new people in her life. The pub was up and running with all the energy and enthusiasm of a new landlord and landlady; workmen and staff were scurrying about and change and excitement were in the air. It must have been a difficult time for Connie but she coped splendidly, with the help of a few therapeutic walks. Gradually her vital place in the scheme of things was worked out and an all-important routine was established.

'Before we started at The Snooty Fox, I called in Health and Safety and explained that Connie would be alerting me to the cooker timer. Now, before customers arrive, Connie is there and alerts me to this. This is usually the time when I work alone in the kitchen, for once customers arrive there are normally staff around to help. I then take Connie upstairs and she has her well-earned rest. This is the only time I am parted from Connie, but as she doesn't like the noise in the kitchen this is probably the best thing to do. Also there are times when we get very busy and it wouldn't do to have her in the way then. In reality it was very difficult for Connie, everything working in opposition to her training.'

However, thanks to her wonderful intelligence and adaptability, she coped well. Her conventional training had been going on apace and she became adept at waking Jenny in the morning.

'Many people who have been there and watched her waking me are enthralled by her actions, which invariably seem to commence with a look that says, "Not that thing again!" Then it's up and out of her basket, which is always situated close to my bed, and, with a stretch and a yawn, it's off to work. Sometimes when she has woken me she goes back to her basket to catch up on her beauty sleep, but I can understand this as my job involves long hours and hence so does hers. I often feel guilty about this, as I am seemingly on the go all the time. Where, then, does she get the chance of a quick nap to recharge her batteries?

'If I am working in the office she does have her place under the desk and always makes a beeline for this when I go in there. Sometimes I let her remain there when I go downstairs. As I go about my day, cooking large amounts of food, the cooker timer is another wonderful assistant. Now I appreciate being able to cook when it suits me and not having to wait for someone to be around to "lend me their ears". Connie is very reliable, but there is something about a working kitchen that frightens her. I can well understand this, for there seem to be noises and precariously placed items all around.'

Connie, having been trained to alert Jenny, found the constant stream of delivery people difficult to handle, especially those carrying large plastic bags. The butcher and the sausage-maker were two of the worst: when they arrived her fur would stand on end and she would bark fiercely, belying her gentle nature, although she never bit anyone. Possibly something happened in her early life to make her afraid.

'The problem has improved as we practised using rattling plastic bags and even putting her treats in them. The bark is still there when delivery men arrive, but I have no intention of curing that as it gives me so much protection and security. The doorbell became her one big headache! Being a pub environment, we offer open house and everyone is welcome, but because they do not ring the doorbell they break every rule in Connie's book and she will bark at them. Especially if they enter by the back way which is rather darker than the front—she sort of sees a vague shape of someone appearing out of the dark.

'We consulted with the Centre about this problem as we felt it was quite offputting to some of our customers, especially the elderly people, to be greeted by a somewhat loud bark. She is a lot better nowadays but she still does it sometimes.'

In the middle of all this excitement, of moving to a new pub, a new business and a new life, the day of Connie's finals arrived far too quickly. Jenny remembers how nervous she was for Connie. It was worse than doing exams herself!

'Tony Blunt came again, and I was pleased about that, as he now had first-hand experience of our two homes, both very similar with hills, lakes and lots of good walking areas.'

He put Connie very thoroughly through her paces, seeing how she reacted to all the sounds she had been trained for. Jenny was so proud of her. She behaved impeccably, and at the end Tony Blunt announced that she had achieved her final grading. She received her yellow coat, lead and collar and Jenny was given a certificate proving that she owned a qualified Hearing Dog for the Deaf. They were on their way!

'Did she look smart! Her dark fur was perfectly offset by the bright yellow coat. Who could fail to notice her?'

It was to be the beginning of a challenging time for them both. Jenny's first official job as a Hearing Dog owner was to visit Bassenthwaite Church of England School, where there was a little deaf boy. The idea was that she could give him some inspiration, help and support. The visit had a very profound effect on Jenny and directed her plans for the future.

'I came away with very deep feelings that he needed help, and it wasn't long before I signed up on a Deaf Awareness course at Carlisle under the tutorship of Celeste Bonifanti. My idea of joining this course was to get it all perfect and then go along to the school to talk to staff and parents, and to bring some understanding of deafness which in turn would prove beneficial to the little deaf boy.'

With Connie beside her, her confidence was growing, and she began to realise the importance of the work that she could do in the Deaf world, acting as a bridge for understanding.

That idea took an unexpected turn when, not long after opening The Snooty Fox, Jenny had a visitor. Alf Frith was deaf and his wife was hearing, and they were staying at a guest-house nearby. One evening they decided to search out the local pub. The guest-house owner asked Alf where he was going, and when he was told they were off to look for somewhere to have a couple of pints, his reply was, 'Why don't you go to The Snooty Fox where there is a deaf landlady with a TALKING DOG?'

Jenny has come across quite a number of variations where the correct title for Hearing Dogs is concerned, but this was a new one for her! Since she acquired Connie, references to Hearing Dogs for Deaf People have included 'guide dogs for the deaf', 'deaf dogs', 'dogs for the hearing', 'listening dogs', and even 'hearing dogs for the blind'.

The 'talking dog' was a bonus, as Alf Frith and his wife were thus led to The Snooty Fox. He turned out to be an ex-Mary Hare Grammar School pupil, although he was older than Jenny. Since, like her, he had a hearing partner, the two hit it off immediately. This couple was the first of many deaf people to visit The Snooty Fox, which quickly became famous across the Deaf community. It was one of the first indications of the many changes that were to take place in Jenny's life. And it was all due to the 'Talking Dog'.

Fourteen

Thanks to Connie, Jenny now had a chance to enjoy her new-found world. For her it was like coming home at last.

Apart from the few schoolfriends she had kept in touch with from the Mary Hare Grammar School, for some thirty years she had been starved of the company of other deaf people. In that time there had been great changes, not only in the provision of modern technology, but in attitudes among both deaf and hearing people. Gone were the days when much was beyond the reach of the deaf: there was now more equality of opportunity with their hearing peers and sign language was becoming more accepted. Connie was to open the door to this new, exciting world.

To Jenny, the sudden realisation that other Deaf people were part of her world, as she was part of theirs, came as a great shock. She began to enjoy sign language and to explore her own identity as a Deaf person. For so long sign language had been a sort of forbidden language for her, due mainly to its associations with Manchester and all her horrific memories of the place. Now, thanks to Connie's support, she began to realise how important it was to be able to communicate with fellow Deaf people, that in the Deaf community she could find perfect understanding and relaxation.

'Why had I been stupid enough to turn my back on these?' she wonders now. 'I feel like celebrating that I have found myself. I have rediscovered my identity and thank heaven that it's not too late to enjoy it, and that it is there to be enjoyed. Thank heaven too that lots of other Deaf people kept this language and culture alive.'

The Snooty Fox not only became increasingly popular with holidaymakers seeking out the lesser known corners of Lakeland, it also quickly became known as the pub where Deaf people could go and meet their friends, and be assured of an understanding welcome. All were made to feel at home in the warm atmosphere, and every one of them in their own way played their part in moulding Jenny's emerging identity.

'Each and all made me look inside myself and find such similarities in our Deaf way of life. They continue to make me feel so surprised whenever I meet these Deaf people, surprised that I have gone along so far and only just realised this fact—that I am part of their world. But they also make me very grateful because they have helped me to find my true self and they have given me such pride in my Deafness.

'My language, which has been suppressed for so long, is now used whenever the occasion presents itself and, unlike previous times in my childhood when I was so ashamed to be seen signing in public, I now sign in joy. Conversations are a happy thing, free from feelings of stress. And I have Connie to thank for all of this! Without the confidence that she has given me, I could never have begun this wonderful journey of self-discovery.

'I have realised how I wish to run my life. It has to be a balance between the two worlds. If I were to be plunged back to that old world full of hearing people I am quite sure I would now go mad! I very much need this combination. It is fortunate that Geoff is so understanding and doesn't try to deprive me of my new-found discovery. He understands my need to be with my own kind. Maybe what he doesn't quite understand, though, is the frenzied rushing about trying to make the whole world aware of Deafness!'

Jenny had always been rather afraid of small children, sharply aware of the communication difficulties which could make mutual understanding a struggle. But with the birth of her first grandchild, Josey, in November 1994, another door was to open.

'Josey knows quite a few signs. I always said I wanted her to learn to sign but I think the whole family seemed to think this useful. Since she is so quick it hasn't been difficult to get her to sign.

'I remember her looking at me very hard when I first signed to her and, like my own children, she has noticed something different about me. She knows she has to tap me if she wants my attention. She has a strong Cumbrian accent and I don't always follow what she says, so it is handy if she can sign.

'She can sign the words for many animals too, and I often ask her in sign if Connie is a "rabbit", "cat" or some other animal, and she signs back to me in disgust, "Nooo! Dog, dog, dog." It is obvious that she is an animal lover and loves Connie, giving her hugs whenever she sees her. At first every dog she saw was called "Connie".

'When Josey gets older and more understanding I am sure we shall be able to converse together, and hopefully she will be the one family member who will be able to talk to me in my own language. I never taught my own children to sign because I had been told time and again to sacrifice my language to be "normal", to talk because I was part of a minority group, and it was far too much to expect others to bow to me. I now know that my children wish I had taught them too, especially at a time when learning would have been so much quicker.

'But I now realise I do have this love of children and it has come to the fore when I meet children who are deaf. I could spend hours chatting to them. I see so many children who miss conversing in their own language in the home and I wish I could spend time with them, giving them this special something—a language we can use with ease. For with language comes knowledge.'

In many other ways Connie's presence became a social asset, giving Jenny confidence in meeting people and helping her to overcome the shyness and fear that had dominated her life for so long.

'My natural love of meeting people had long been suppressed—with hearing people mainly through fear of the unknown: not knowing, if I spoke to someone, whether I'd be able to understand them. In the past I have also been aware of people being afraid of not being able to understand me, and those who did confront me and were told that I was deaf were liable to make an immediate exit! Some would insist on talking to me even though they were impossible to understand, and then my responses became dependent on body language and facial expressions. I could then only reply in monosyllables for fear of saying the wrong thing. Some (and my own mother was in this group) would begin a conversation fully aware of my deafness but lose awareness halfway through. One had to keep reminding them to slow down. Others would talk to me behind my back or when I was looking elsewhere and would then think me rude or appear puzzled when I didn't reply. And there were others who were good conversers with the deaf or were deaf themselves, who would have spoken to me had they only known.'

All this has changed now for Jenny. The distinctive yellow coat is a giveaway to her Deafness. Or is it? Some people have the mistaken idea that her dog is deaf, and she is often asked if the dog can understand sign language. This last is a sensible question. In fact, if Jenny's voice had been unclear, Connie would have been taught by the Hearing Dog Centre to respond to signs. However, as Jenny has good speech, Connie has been taught to understand spoken commands.

It is a surprisingly common misconception that Connie

can talk, as the proprietor of the guest-house who directed Alf Frith and his wife to The Snooty Fox obviously thought. Jenny's funniest experience of the public's reaction to that yellow coat was on a summer's day in Keswick. She was enjoying a break from shopping, walking Connie in Fitz Park, the beautiful riverside gardens which are a feature of this Lake District town. Set under the great bulk of Skiddaw, and with the River Greta leaping joyfully alongside its lawns, it is a lovely place to stroll in winter or summer. Connie, on the lead, was enjoying herself, trotting along sniffing the warm air and the intriguing smells, while Jenny admired the rhododendrons ablaze by the foaming river. Where else could one escape from the grind of bulk shopping at Caterite and be in surroundings like this in five minutes?

She was just counting her blessings when she felt a tap on her shoulder. She swung round, startled. There was an elderly woman standing at her elbow, obviously chattering nineteen to the dozen, pointing to Connie's coat and looking rather put out that Jenny had ignored her completely. Jenny shook her head and explained in a loud voice that she was profoundly deaf and couldn't hear her at all, tempering the explanation with one of her beaming smiles. Understanding dawned! The elderly woman nodded enthusiastically, patting Jenny's arm kindly by way of reassurance. Then, clutching her handbag to her bosom, she bent down to where Connie was sitting patiently on the path. Carefully, she lined her face up with Connie's until they were staring at one another, eye to eye. Connie pushed her black muzzle forward and gave the old woman's hand a tentative lick. But not to be distracted, and mouthing very carefully so that there was no possibility of misunderstanding, the woman shouted to the surprised dog: 'CAN YOU ASK YOUR OWNER HOW OLD YOU ARE?'

Incidents like this can lighten the day but, misunderstandings apart, there are enormous advantages to the yellow coat. Deaf people come up to Jenny, knowing that she too is deaf. Many hearing people stop her to ask about Connie. They are meeting her halfway, knowing they will have to be prepared for any communication problems, and Jenny finds she is given valuable help with things she was never aware of before. She is also now able to deal good-humouredly with situations that she would once have found embarrassing or demeaning. I saw that in action one day when we had been out together and was much moved by it.

'She speaks very well,' said the woman in the pub where we stopped for lunch on the way home, meaning to be kind. Jenny smiled her beatific smile and replied:

'Thank you, thank you very much.'

'No, I mean it,' said the woman slowly and carefully, still addressing me. 'Lots of them don't, you know. I don't know how she does it. And you are so patient. Do you have sign language?'

'No, I don't,' I said. 'Jenny lip-reads me.'

She turned to Jenny.

'Oh, you are patient too. It must be very difficult.'

Rather irritated by this patronising attitude, which Jenny deflected with so much courtesy, I announced:

'Jenny owns and runs a very famous pub in the Lake District.'

A variety of emotions galloped across the woman's face. It was a briefly satisfying moment. After a few more minutes of chatting, Jenny's vibrant personality had made another convert to Deaf Awareness and I was left feeling I had a lot to learn.

'How would I manage without Connie now?' Jenny said as we continued our journey. 'She is such a vitally important part of my life. Twice I have almost suffered from a heart attack thinking I'd lost her. The first time was when I was shopping in Carlisle. She is so well trained out of the house that there is really no need to use the lead—indeed, she works much better without it—it's just for safety's sake. On this occasion I turned round to look at her in the crowded town, only to discover that I was walking around with a lead and collar and no dog. I had wondered why people were staring at me!

'A quick rush back to the previous store, quite sick with worry, my heart pounding. I confronted the security guard, holding up the empty lead and collar and asking, "Have you seen my dog?" He called up another security guard and they consulted together. It was obvious that they had never had this sort of problem to deal with before. I was getting these hot and cold flushes and was really desperate. Just as one of the guards got out his pad for details, along came a woman saying there was a dog waiting by the very stall I had last been looking at!

'The second time was when I arrived back after a long journey. She knew she was home and jumped out immediately I opened the car door. I didn't know this and looked in the back for her, to find her not there. Visions of leaving her at the motorway service station where we last stopped ran through my mind, along with those hot and cold flushes again. It was a living death—how was I going to tell the Hearing Dog Centre that I had lost my dog?

'I cried aloud, "Oh Connie, where are you?" and that wonderful cold nose touched my hand. I could live again!'

Fifteen

One day in The Snooty Fox, Jenny started chatting to a couple who were walking the Cumbria Way, and was intrigued by their descriptions of the route. The Cumbria Way is an 'unofficial route' through Cumbria which was brought into being through the concerted efforts of the Ramblers' Association. Seventy miles long, and running from Ulverston, close to the shores of Morecambe Bay in the south of the county, through the beautiful Lake District National Park to the border city of Carlisle in the north, it is a wonderful way of getting to know the real Lakeland away from the madding crowd, although, like the Dales way, it is a route which lies rather more in the valleys than on the fell summits. Jenny was inspired, and began to think about the possibility of taking up the challenge of the walk with Connie. It would be quite an endurance test for them both, but a good way of testing themselves for the longer walk which Jenny had dreamt of doing to raise money for Hearing Dogs.

'I went about making enquiries and managed to rope my daughter Kerry in. Kerry really got the positive action going by saying, "I've booked some time off work, so it's now or never!"'

Kerry is very experienced in the necessary skills of map–reading and route-planning. That at least was a comfort, but having made the big decision, Jenny's main concern was Connie. She consulted with Hearing Dogs about how best to look after her. Would it be too long a distance? After all, she didn't want to risk her in any way. Hearing Dogs were very reassuring, but she was flooded with advice from well-meaning friends about how best to look after Connie's welfare during this arduous journey—to take along some surgical spirit for her paws, and what sort of special food ration she would need. The more she heard, the more nervous Jenny became. What were they taking on?

The great day—25th October—dawned with frantic preparations at The Snooty Fox. There were the usual Sunday lunches to prepare, as well as rucksacks to be packed, spare socks to be counted, boots (well broken-in), chocolate bars, emergency food and, most importantly, rations for Connie, to be assembled. Connie seemed to sense that some sort of special 'walkies' was on the horizon, and spent the day getting in the way, sticking her nose into the rucksacks, where that mysterious and appetising smell of food seemed to be lurking. What was going on? Her food had been weighed out and distributed between their backpacks, but even so would be a considerable weight. There was some consolation, though, that the further they walked, the lighter would be the load.

On one point Connie was determined: she wasn't going to be left behind, even though that meant getting in the hated car. Geoff had offered to drive Jenny and Kerry down to Ulverston that night so that they would be ready to begin the next morning, and as they were packing up the car Connie, quite uncharacteristically, jumped in and sat among the rucksacks, wagging her tail and looking straight ahead with an air of anticipation. She, at least, had no doubts.

What could be more beautiful than the Lake District in early autumn? A clear, golden day with the colours on the trees preternaturally sharp. Jenny reflected how lucky they were, after all these years, to have ended up living here, in such a perfect spot. She was so fortunate.

As they drove through the Lakes, the reds and greens, russets and golds of leaves on the ancient oaks and beeches, and the dappled shadow on the white farm-houses, seemed to set fire to the landscape. Blue lakes mirrored the tawny colours of the fells. It was the end of a walking weekend for many visitors. Families with ruck-sacks, big and small, were coming to the end of the day; children trailed along behind, tired and ready for bed, their parents looking rather footsore. Yet they all seemed happy and even sunburnt from the October sun, and from the fresh wind which almost always blows on the summits. Jenny couldn't help wondering how weary she might be by the end of the next day.

It seemed a very long way down to Ulverston ... past Bassenthwaite and the old grey town of Keswick, with late-blooming roses in higgledy-piggledy gardens, brooded over by grey Skiddaw; down past great Helvellyn and the forested shores of Thirlmere, shadowed and mysterious, its glowing depths reflecting the autumn colours of the trees. Jenny and Kerry sat quietly in the car while Geoff drove, looking at the beauties of the countryside and thinking about the next day's challenge.

As the car climbed up the pass on Dunmail Raise, more weary walkers were coming down the steep rocky path from Grizedale Tarn. It had been a hot day on the tops for the time of year, yet next week the fells might well be dusted by the first snows of winter—you could never tell in the Lakes. Jenny hoped the cold weather would hold off for a few more days at any rate. They were hardly equipped for snow, even if they were to avoid the tops. Sunburn they could cope with! The weather was always so capricious in the Lakes that thermals and waterproofs as well as suncream had had to be packed. In some ways the Lakeland weather was almost the biggest challenge of all.

As if to echo Jenny's thoughts, a yellow Sea King Moun-tain Rescue helicopter came blundering up the pass like a giant, ungainly bird, finally disappearing over the slopes of Helvellyn. Someone, somewhere had pushed themselves too far or slipped on the path in unsuitable footware. It was an environment which, for all its loveliness, needed to be treated with respect.

Grasmere and Ambleside were still crowded with evening visitors, the lake secret and still in the autumn dusk. A swan was gliding across Rydal Water as they passed, perfectly reflected in the mirror of the water. Jenny felt a sudden longing to be out there, amongst the fells, walking, away from the crowds and coaches which clogged the lakeside roads even at this time of the year. It would be fun! And she would have Connie and Kerry for company. She was really looking forward to it . . . and it was all part of her new, positive attitude.

Yet, the farther they drove, the more she became convinced they would never make that long, long walk. They had planned to finish in Keswick at the end of three days, but it still felt a very long way. What had she taken on? After driving down the winding road to Coniston, they finally arrived at their bed and breakfast accommodation in the little market town of Ulverston—the southern end of the Cumbria Way. They would have about a mile to go to the start of the walk in the morning, and then it would be full steam ahead.

Connie went straight to sleep in her basket beside Jenny's bed, but Jenny herself lay awake for a while, wondering what tomorrow would bring. It hardly seemed a moment before she felt the soft tap of Connie's paw on her arm, and when she peeped through the curtains it was barely light outside. Kerry was already awake and in the bathroom. At least it wasn't raining! They ate a hearty breakfast to keep them going through the day, provided by the friendly couple who ran the bed and breakfast hotel. Connie was tremendously excited, and as they set off with her on the lead down the first mile towards the start of the Cumbria Way, she had a real spring in her step, her fronded tail wagging wildly. This was going to be a really special walk.

The Way began in a large car park where a sign—'Gillbanks, Start of the Cumbria Way'—indicated the route. A metalled path followed the rushing beck which, despite the recently dry weather, was still chuckling along merrily, sparkling in the early morning sunshine. The beck had provided much of the water power to the mills in the days when Ulverston was a textile centre. They set off with a will, and when they had got away from the road they were able to let Connie off the lead for a welcome gallop. Jenny was to find in the days to come that Connie was the least of their problems: she couldn't have been happier. This was her idea of doggy heaven and she never showed the smallest sign of being tired or out of sorts. It was a lovely morning, a wonderful feeling to be alone, supporting each other, walking close to nature and appreciating the beauties all around them.

Jenny gloried in the wonderful colours of the woods as they walked up into the fells. Although she couldn't hear the sound of the beck, she could see the dancing light on the water as it splashed over boulders in the river bed and cascaded over miniature waterfalls. There were still flowers starring the grassy banks, and above them was the brilliant blue sky of a fine October day, contrasting with the rich tapestry of colours from the oaks and beeches on the fellside slopes. But it would take a bit of time for their stiff muscles to get into shape! Jenny's legs felt like lead to start with on the uphill stretches, and she had trouble keeping up with Kerry. Connie had no such problems. From the beginning she loved every minute of it, skipping and rolling about, her tail wagging furiously. She would gallop a few yards up the path, and then stop and look back with impatience as though to say, 'What's keeping you two?' She was in her element.

Up and down through the undulating countryside of

the South Lakes, they walked on, occasionally stopping for a snack. But it was not long before the awful realisation dawned—they had brought nothing to drink! They had imagined they would at least be passing through a village where they could buy something, but the path carefully avoided all but the most isolated farms. They were destined to get very thirsty indeed.

There were still sheep on the fells, not yet brought down by the farmers for the 'tupping' season. It wouldn't be long, however, before they would be gathered in for the attention of the ram, and already on the fellside slopes, amongst the tawny bracken, they could see small flocks of sheep being herded up by the fell farmers and their sheep dogs and that new phenomenon of the Lakeland fells, the motorised tractor bike. They passed small, white-painted farmhouses, with other dogs sleeping in the sun, who opened one eye as they passed and then fell back to sleep. Everywhere there were splashes of brightness, not only in the translucent colours of the trees, but in geraniums on black-painted window-sills, red chrysanthemums in fellside gardens, and even the occasional walker clad in day-glo orange and purple. Farms and churches, great grey boulders, sheep, and little woods and sparkling waterfalls, all under a blue sky. It was heaven!

Eventually, after what seemed like many miles, they dropped down to a bridge over a beck and then, after another climb, to Beacon Tarn where they felt they could have a rest and some well-deserved nourishment. How they longed for a drink! At least Connie had been able to lap at streams on the way, but mindful of advice about liver flukes and dead sheep upstream, they dared not follow her example. Jenny splashed her hot face gratefully in the icy water.

The Way continued along the western shore of the tarn and through a depression at the far end. Ahead there was a steep drop to a marshy area with no clear tracks. Jenny and Connie both got muddy feet. Although there had been no rain for a while it was still very wet and there was no really clear path. Eventually, after floundering about for a while, they found a path off to the west. Thank goodness for Kerry's skilled map-reading!

A few more miles brought them to the beck which flowed out of Torver Tarn. There is something about tarns that makes one want to stop and linger, especially as by then they were very tired; Connie, however, still looked as though she could go on for ever.

By now Jenny's feet were really sore and she was glad of the extra pair of socks that she had put on inside her walking boots. Most important of all, she had actually walked her boots in properly. They followed a clear track down the left-hand side of the valley to the foot-bridge, and after crossing the road at last saw, to their relief, the sign 'Coniston via Lake Shore'.

The lake lay blue and tranquil under the late afternoon sun. The road was busy, and seeing so many tourists with their cars parked alongside the lake was a shock after the peaceful hours in the fells. Somehow the sight of the lake, with its forested shores and little islands, and even a pair of geese skimming over its surface, gave them a new lease of life, and Jenny was able to walk on with a will. Connie decided it was time to have a bath and splashed about in the shallows along the lake shore. She was happy!

The track finished at Coniston Hall, and as they walked up into the old green-slated town Jenny realised that she was desperately aching, tired and footsore. It had been a long day and now, as the sun slipped down behind the fells, it was becoming dark and quite cold. Wearily they trudged through Coniston in search of their guest-house. They were, by now, seriously dehydrated—that was a mistake they would not make the next day. All Jenny wanted was to collapse into a hot bath, and to be greeted with the notice 'showers only to be taken' was a ghastly shock.

'We just *had* to ignore this message and a bath with Radox quite restored us! We realised how silly we had been to walk that far without anything to drink as we had thought we would be able to buy some along the way. Were we expecting to see Sainsbury's on top of the Langdales? But the result was we couldn't face much food.'

Once again, the next morning, after a refreshing sleep, Jenny was woken by the gentle touch of Connie's paw. To her surprise, after testing her limbs gingerly, she found that she was actually free of aches and pains and was mentally really looking forward to the day's walking. She could feel her fitness coming back already, and as for Connie, she couldn't wait to get started.

Mindful this time to fill up their flasks before they started, they ate a huge breakfast and set off along the second section of the route which led from Coniston via Tarn Hows, Skelwith Bridge and Elterwater to Dungeon Ghyll at the foot of the Langdales. It was to prove a long day, and in some ways quite tiring, for this stretch of the Way was very close to civilisation. At one stage they found themselves on the edge of a quarry, having to avoid giant lorries, and they had to cross a number of roads which meant putting Connie back on the lead and keeping a sharp eye open for tourist traffic. All the while, as they climbed steadily, they were aware of coming closer and closer to the spectacular Langdale Pikes which seemed to beckon them on. Nevertheless it was a hard day, and the last little stretch, as they crossed beside Elterwater and made their way up into the enclosed valley under the Langdale Pikes, seemed very long indeed. At least this time they had been able to stop for drink as well as food! By the time the three of them reached the path beside the River Brathay, Jenny was exhausted.

'We arrived at Dungeon Ghyll late in the afternoon and I was literally all in. We came upon the New Dungeon Ghyll Hotel, only to be told the Old Dungeon Ghyll Hotel, which we had booked into, was a good mile down the road. I had to call upon every last ounce of strength to walk this distance and I was getting quite angry with myself, fearing that I was going to have to give up. To be honest, my muscles and everything else had gone and I had difficulty mounting the stairs. But the blessed Radox bath beckoned!'

Jenny was also cheered by a chance meeting in the lobby of the hotel. As they walked in, with Connie in her bright yellow Hearing Dog coat, three young men who had been sitting there reading a magazine looked up, and their mouths literally dropped open. Excitedly, they came crowding round Connie and explained that they had been reading an article about Hearing Dogs, which they proceeded to show Jenny and Kerry.

'When Connie walked in, in all her splendour, showing off as always when wearing her yellow coat, the lads thought the magazine had come alive! It was a laugh to see them gaping, but I initially thought it was because of me, with my funny walk! I was so stiff I could hardly walk straight.'

The Old Dungeon Ghyll is a traditional Lakeland hotel, renowned as the birthplace of Mountain Rescue in the Langdales. Owned by Sid Cross and his wife, it became a magnet for climbers wishing to explore the challenges of the Langdale Valley. From the informal rescue teams which helped each other out in case of accident, the famous Langdale/Ambleside Mountain Rescue Team was born, of which Sid Cross, now in his eighties, is still the President.

Once more they slept the sleep of the just. Jenny had been so stiff by the end of the walk that she had really begun to wonder if she would be able to carry on, although Connie was still springing about like a young lamb and Kerry hardly looked tired at all. Next day, however, a miracle happened.

'All the aches and pains vanished and I am convinced Radox had a lot to be thanked for. There was pleasure also to realise this long last trek to the hotel had lessened the distance for the next stint. But all this was quite forgotten when we viewed the route from afar and saw the eternally winding path to be tackled up into the Langdales. Negative thoughts crept in, especially as the mist began to descend.'

This was indeed the toughest section of the walk. From behind the Old Dungeon Ghyll, the path climbed in front of them steeply, up to the wide head of Great Langdale, better known as Mickleden. The jagged mountainous face was enough to strike fear in the heart—it looked so steep! What was worse was that, unlike the other days, which had been sunny, the mist lay in wisps all across the upper parts of the valley, and as they climbed upwards the sun quite literally went out. Wild country indeed, unlike the pretty Lakeland scenery of the lower valleys. Sere grass, patches of boggy ground, huge grey boulders which looked as though they had been tipped there by the careless hand of some passing giant, and tumbled rocks that spoke of the glaciers which had carved this spectacular landscape. All this was hardly comforting as the grey, cold mist came down. Jenny found herself getting slower and slower and Kerry, glancing upwards nervously at the mist as it slowly sank down into the valley, did her best to encourage her.

'Kerry was very concerned and did her best to hurry me on the way. She even took my backpack to lessen my load. All I got from Connie, always ahead, was a frustrated look at my slowness. She seemed so impatient to see what was on the other side of the mountain . . . and so say all of us!'

Jenny was grateful to see that, to ease the strain, there were zigzags all the way up the path. She reflected that some poor packhorse had probably had to stagger up here at some time. Even with Kerry taking her backpack she

148

knew how those poor horses must have felt. At the end of the valley, beyond a wooden footbridge, a guide stone indicated that a path led up Stake Pass. The glaciation of the valley meant that the upper slopes were steeper than those lower down, and the climb became correspondingly hard.

The mist had now come down with a vengeance and it was hard to see more than a few feet in front of them. Jenny summoned up all her last strength and, encouraged by Connie and Kerry, at last made it to the top of the pass. Connie came bounding back, tail wagging, and rewarded her with a lick. She stopped completely out of breath and suddenly, as happens so often in the Lake District, the mist lifted as though swept aside by the same giant hand which had been dropping boulders everywhere. Larks rose up from the heather, a pair of wheatears fluttered on a group of stones. As they trudged on they saw in front of them the most wonderful sight—a plateau of golden gorse glowing in the October sun, crowning the pass in the midst of that arid landscape.

After that the way became a lot easier and at last they felt they were nearing Keswick and familiar ground. There was a long walk down Langstrath with its bouldery path, but once again they were cheered by the nearness of cascading water, as the river leaped beside them in waterfalls and pools, a familiar friend encouraging them on. Gradually the bare landscape of the high glacial valley gave way to woods and trees and the soft airs of the lower slopes. It was so lovely to be going downhill at last. They reached the bottom of the valley and walked up Borrowdale, suddenly quite glad to be seeing tourists and traffic again. Their first glimpse of Keswick was almost immediately obliterated by black clouds scudding up the valley, and a torrential downpour which soaked them even before they had time to put on their waterproofs. The only comfort was that at least it hadn't rained on top of Stake Pass.

'I do have to say what a brilliant navigator Kerry was,' Jenny remembers warmly. 'She guided us all the way with just a small book. We only took the wrong direction once. There are two things we learned—to take a good map and drinks wherever you go.'

There in the car park was the welcome face of Geoff, greeting the two poor drowned rats and a very wet Connie. Oh, for a very, very long Radox bath, and a hot drink and a long sleep. Connie, sitting wetly in the back of the car on the journey home, had other ideas. Her eager expression, as she peered out at the sodden landscape, seemed to say, 'That was a nice little walk! Can we do another one tomorrow?'

At the end of the journey Jenny looks back and ponders, 'What was all that fuss about Connie? She had loved every minute of it and skipped and rolled a lot of the way. She was so energetic. What about poor me? I found I had muscles where I never knew muscles were, and I certainly experienced how they can ache!'

Sixteen

Since walking the Cumbria Way Kerry, on her own, has accomplished the Coast to Coast Walk in reverse, starting at Robin Hood's Bay in Yorkshire and finishing on the Cumbrian coast at St Bees. She did this in only twelve days and Jenny is proud of her achievement, but she is sure that Kerry missed the companionship of Connie and the sheer pleasure of seeing a dog enjoying herself so much. For Connie, walks are the high points of her life, and even when she is at her busiest Jenny always finds time to indulge her.

'There are many times when I find myself burdened with so much work and I think I'll skip the walks, but she looks at me with such pleading eyes that I always give in. I know this is the least I can do for her for all she does for me. Once we reach the fields then it's freedom time for her. She responds so well to the whistle recall and returns every time. On several occasions she has had flocks of sheep following.

'I always come out of it better too. Once the wind off the fells blows through my hair, any stress and depression just vanish. Come rain or shine, I get so much enjoyment from the countryside. You will often find me and my dog skipping along, and maybe I will be humming an old school song—out of tune no doubt, but feeling content-ment for all I have. In this busy age it is so easy to let go and not bother, so it's wonderful to have Connie who gets me out, keeping me healthier both physically and mentally.'

Sometimes Jenny feels that she is trying to make up

for lost time, for all those years when her Deafness was smothered. So when Cumbria Deaf Association asked her if she would like to tutor a little boy in sign language she jumped at the opportunity.

'When I thought about it I wondered, why me? My signing has only just come into being and many of my signs are from my childhood days in Manchester and have been lying dormant for years.' Even so, she was excited by the challenge.

As soon as she set eyes on her new pupil she realised, with her highly developed sensitivity to body language and signs, that he wasn't deaf but that he would never be able to talk and so needed signs to communicate.

'Every visit brought achievements, some small, some large, but all gave me immense inspiration. I have seen with my own eyes the enormity of the problem that hearing people face when confronted with a deaf child.'

Jenny became aware that Deaf people like herself could play a vital role in helping parents to understand their deaf children, so that they would be equipped to cope in the hearing world. She knew from her own experience how hard it was to manage in an oral, aural environment, particularly in further education where the stresses were bad enough for those who could hear, without the additional problems of deafness. She wanted to do what she could to help parents, who know their children best, to create a close family group by developing fluent communication within it through the medium of sign language.

'I visited Bristol University to see for myself their successful project "Deaf Child at Home" and was able to visit the group attached to the school at the Family Centre. The highlight of this visit was to see the nursery school children, many as young as three years old, conversing in sign, full of confidence and expression. They had no hesitation in sitting beside me and chatting away to me. It made me so enthralled.'

The visit was an inspiration that led to a huge widening of her horizons. While still playing a full role at The Snooty Fox, she started working for East Lancashire Deaf Society to develop their 'Bridging the Gap' project. Her aim was to create something similar to the Bristol scheme—a place where families could learn from Deaf adults, many of whom have never experienced a real family life, mainly because hearing people have never had it explained to them what it means to be deaf, by the very people who know. Jenny could now look back on her own childhood with fresh understanding.

'My own mother did everything the people in authority or in professions told her to do, even though many of these must have been against her instinct. Why else did she persist in taking me to the Manchester school despite seeing the immense unhappiness this wrought in me? How could she pick me up every Friday evening and return me on Sunday evenings and then travel back via a bus, a train and another bus, a slow journey in those days, alone and with her memory of being wrenched apart from me—I had pleaded with her not to leave me there. She must have been so unhappy herself, but she must also have been convinced that this was what was best for me.

'Parents have much more choice today, but how can they make reasoned choices without unbiased information? Their children will also reap the rewards of meeting Deaf adults and seeing what they can do and have done in their lives, how they can drive a car or buy a house—all everyday things that many people think they cannot do.

'It is not only born deaf children or severely/profoundly deaf children who need help and understanding, but also children who have a slight hearing loss because the true extent of their deafness may not be recognised. Many of them are expected to function as hearing children, which places an enormous burden on them.

'There are new approaches to be learnt—touching for attention, eye contact and so much body language to understand—but if we work as one happy team, all this learning will become a wonderful experience. Deaf children too, who may never have met Deaf adults and so never had a role model, find they can ask questions. Many believe that when they are grown-up they will be hearing, and it is important to prepare them properly for adulthood in the Deaf world.

'I must always remember that this new world for me has really come about through Connie. It is Connie who has brought about my independence, self-esteem and sense of security. She protects me and looks after me in so many ways. It is that same four-legged wonder who advertises my Deafness and hence gives me the introductions to people who understand and to the many new deaf friends I have made. Without this bright yellow coat the help that is on hand would never be given.'

*　　*　　*

The WI in Lower Fellside were used to visiting speakers, but this occasion was different: there was an air of tension and anxiety in the village hall. The Chairwoman, Mrs Tallentire, had bravely gone out on a limb, writing to the deaf owner of a Hearing Dog to ask her to come to talk. Outside it was thick fog and very cold. Mrs Tallentire grew more anxious. The business part of the meeting had almost finished and still there was no sign of Mrs Harmer. Could she even drive? Mrs Tallentire had not thought to ask in her letter how Mrs Harmer was going to get to the meeting. And when she got there, would she even be able to talk to the members, so that they would understand? After all, nobody in Lower Fellside and its surrounding, isolated hamlets had even a smattering of sign language. Mrs Tallentire began to feel she might have made a rash decision.

154

Yet the article she had read in the local paper had been intriguing. Mrs Harmer was a very independent lady, so it said in the *Cumberland News*, who owned a pub with her husband and, despite a busy life, was raising thousands of pounds for the charity Hearing Dogs for Deaf People. There was a picture. Mrs Harmer was the first person in Cumbria to have a Hearing Dog and she often talked to local groups to raise money for her charity. Mrs Tallentire (perhaps rushing in where angels feared to tread) had immediately fired off a letter to The Snooty Fox, the pub mentioned in the article, asking Mrs Harmer to come and talk, and even to bring the dog. Had it been wise after all?

The door opened, letting in some of the dank fog that hung around the village hall like an old grey ghost. One or two elderly members shivered slightly, drawing their cardigans around them. Then there was a cheery shout and a small woman, radiating energy, strode beaming into the hall, dressed in a navy tracksuit and trainers and preceded by a black dog. The dog was wearing a yellow coat and wagging its fronded tail. The woman flicked brown curly hair out of her eyes with an impatient gesture, while with one hand she hung on to the dog lead. A box of slides was tucked under her arm.

'Hello, everyone!'

Her speech was quite clear. Mrs Tallentire felt a surge of relief. By now everyone's attention had shifted to the other member of the team; an audible 'Ah' rippled through the audience. Deep-set brown eyes looked a little anxiously from side to side, while the black dog pulled on the lead, paws slipping slightly on the polished surface of the hall (buffed up specially by the ladies of the committee for Friday's Farmer's Ball).

Too small for a Golden Retriever, the dog looked more like a black collie. There were ripples of gold in the depths of the lustrous coat. She was a beautiful dog, her darkness set off by a bright yellow jacket emblazoned with the slogan HEARING DOG FOR DEAF PEOPLE.

One or two of the braver members reached out and gave the soft coat a stroke. The dog turned and looked, her tail waving gently, before pulling forward once more on the lead.

Jenny turned towards her audience. The dog, following some inner compulsion, moved from where she was sitting and came to sit right by her mistress's ankles, looking up at her with adoring eyes. Jenny Harmer gave her audience an enormous smile which warmed the room in an instant.

'She's a bonny-looking lass,' someone whispered. 'She doesn't look deaf!'

'Thank you for asking me to talk to you this evening. I've been so looking forward to it.'

The audience visibly relaxed. Communication had begun.

'I'm going to tell you a bit about Hearing Dogs and something of my life before I had Connie. Perhaps at the end you will understand how desperately important it is that as many deaf people as possible have a Hearing Dog of their own. For me it is quite simply my lifeline into the hearing world. But, far more than that, I feel she has given me back my life! You see, without Connie, life was lonely and isolated, despite my loving family. It's thanks to Connie that I have the confidence to come here today. I owe so much to her, as you will hear . . . then perhaps when I have told you my story, you will begin to understand.

'For years I was known only by my number. It was tattooed on my wrist! I will never forget it. For years I lost my identity. Only now, thanks to Connie, can I be a truly independent person. But that number, 223, will haunt me for ever. When I look back on my life I can hardly believe it all, and how lucky I am now I have found a friend like Connie—my lifeline.'

The dog looked up, seeming to understand, and licked the outstretched hand.

'You see, unless you are deaf, it is impossible to understand how cut off you feel. After all, to all appearances I look the same as you. Deafness is the hidden disability . . .'

Epilogue

A summer and most of a winter had passed since Jenny and I decided to write this book. Now it was a sharp frosty morning in early February and we had met high on the fell above Uldale for a photo session. As with any occasion which involved Jenny and Connie, it had been a riot of laughter and good-humoured misunderstanding from the beginning. We had minicommed each other early in the morning because the light was good, although clouds were on the horizon. Winter days are very short in Cumbria, and we had to grab what bright moments we could before the shadows grew long once more and the dusk came down.

This was in sharp contrast to the wonderful long summer evenings which seem to go on all night, luminous light never leaving the sky. Some of our pictures had been taken then, but we couldn't seem to get the right one of Connie. She is so black, absorbing light into her coat. It is easy when the sun is in the wrong direction for Connie to end up looking like a black blob.

A wave of mountain bikers in their brightly coloured gear swept past us, one or two of them wobbling a little as they negotiated the icy slope down into the village. Nevertheless, they couldn't resist a wave and a few good-natured comments at the rather unusual sight of two middle-aged ladies, accompanied by a very excited black dog in a yellow coat, and two black labradors with half a mountain each in their mouths, who were providing free entertainment on the slopes above the road.

'Come bye! You two don't look like shepherds!'

This in reference to the large flock of Swaledale sheep which had gathered round us, posing on the skyline, hopeful of extra grub. It was probably too early for the farmer to have been out to dump their hay ration. Not at all put off by the three dogs (who were in any case perfectly sheep-proof and ignored them), they thought we might signal breakfast.

There were some ironic wolf whistles and much good-natured laughter from the bikers as they sped off down the steep hill with the sharp bend at the bottom.

After our minicom conversation I had rushed through the fells to The Snooty Fox, a twenty-minute drive across the moorland road. Jenny had been still in her working whites, dashing about with a huge bunch of keys. Unwisely, I had tried to give her directions to the place where we could meet up (why hadn't I thought to put that in the minicom conversation? It would have been so much easier). Eventually, after misunderstanding each other once or twice, we had agreed to meet on the fell up towards Caldbeck—'Just look for my car by the side of the road!' I had driven off, thinking I could give my dogs a run and set up a perfect site.

Twenty-five minutes later I was still staring at the Swaledales, freezing cold and rather glad of the unsuitable fur fabric jacket I was wearing, with its fleece lining. Where on earth was Jenny? Had I not made myself clear enough? If only I had learnt to sign and wasn't so useless at it! My car was parked by the side of the road at the bottom. Surely we couldn't have missed each other.

I shouted out loud in frustration to the empty skyline with its silent mountains. Then, suddenly, I caught sight of a tiny dot, far down the valley, climbing over the humps of the glacial outwashed sands and gravels which make this strange landscape of the fells above Uldale. Jenny hadn't brought her car! I couldn't believe it! The pub was due to open in about three-quarters of an hour. How on earth would we get the photos done in time? In despair I saw that huge masses of cloud had obscured the summit of Skiddaw. The light had changed from brilliant sunshine with a few tasteful clouds in an intensely blue sky, to a wash of grey which threatened to envelop the horizon. This is what it is like in the fells, and why it is so difficult to take reliable photographs, although when one does catch the light just right, it is stunning.

At last Jenny and I met up with each other. She was gasping for breath and grinning. In response to my half-signed question of 'Why on earth didn't you drive?' she fell about laughing, saying she had no idea I wanted to go so far!

I led Jenny up the fell and showed her where I thought we would get the best light, before teetering off down the steep slope while she struggled with the recalcitrant Connie. We began a hilarious twenty minutes in the freezing wind, with Jenny keeping up a stream of one-liners which had me in fits. Connie was being rather naughty. She was highly excited by this break in her normal Sunday morning routine and refused to behave. She kept lying on her back, expecting her tummy to be tickled, rubbing her head against the short, sheep-cropped grass. Worse, she threatened to coat her shining fur in the liberal scattering of sheep droppings (trunlins, in the local dialect) which peppered the fell. Eventually we made her pay attention and sit up, but she was still being silly, facing into the wind and wanting to play. My two dogs, thankfully, kept out of shot and concentrated on picking up enormous rocks, letting them go in order to watch them roll down the steeper edge of the fellside, uncomfortably close to me. They were jealous of the attention Connie was getting and wanted a bit for themselves.

At last we had done. Connie took off like a young goat, galloping down the fell with her tail in the wind. Jenny shook her head as she caught sight of the huge stones that my dogs were holding in their mouths, tails swishing as they waited to dump them in the back of my Volvo.

'What on earth are those dogs doing? No wonder the level of the mountains is going down!'

The dogs looked at her reproachfully with their doe eyes and carried on wagging their tails. Jenny and Connie were jammed into the front with me, to save Connie being bullied, and we shot back down the fell. We screeched into the car park of The Snooty Fox and Jenny looked at her watch.

'Help! It's half-past eleven. I haven't even done the potatoes. Everyone is going to be waiting for their lunch today!'

We gave each other a hug and Jenny sprinted off at top speed, rather windblown and with Connie's muddy pawmarks all over her coat.

That afternoon I drove back to The Snooty Fox to return some slides. It was late, and a spectacular sunset flared against icy storm clouds over the Lakeland fells. At the highest point I could see across to the Solway where the sky was washed clean, greenish with a hint of rose. The distant firth flashed icy light, the clear sky above auguring frost. It was wild and lonely.

As darkness fell I negotiated the car down the steep slope, over the cattle grid. There were the lights of The Snooty Fox in the centre of Uldale, surrounded by squares of glowing colour from the curtained windows of the whitewashed cottages. The road was slippery with frozen mud.

The back door to The Snooty Fox was locked, so I walked round to the front. Through a tiny window I could see two animated figures, half-signing, half-talking to one another across an empty table in the dining-room. One of them was Jenny. I banged on the window and her companion nudged her. Jenny peered out into the dark, suddenly realising it was me. Her face lit up—a warm feeling; I felt welcome. I walked round to the back with my box of slides and she unlocked the door. The bar was almost in darkness. Connie barked at me wildly and then, realising who it was, wagged her tail and put her delicate black nose in my hand, offering me a sly, warm lick.

'This is my daughter, Kerry,' Jenny said. 'I forgot to tell you she was coming up today from Wales. You know she lives in our cottage at Plas Coch? She's on an Outward Bound Course up here.'

I looked up at the tall, beautiful girl who was smiling at me. She was so like Jenny.

'I've heard all about you,' she said, winking at me and grinning. I wondered what Jenny had been saying.

We sat in the empty bar laughing together. I was due home to cook a meal for my family, but there was so much catching up to do. It is a strange feeling, knowing someone else's life and sharing it with another. I felt immediately close to Kerry, who has an extraordinary serenity about her. Jenny had told me that Kerry, who is now in her twenties, is going deaf and now needs a hearing aid. I didn't like to mention it in case it was still a sensitive subject, but looking at her glowing face it kept jumping into my mind. The reasons are linked to a hereditary gene, the doctors think, but as Jenny still has no knowledge of her real parents, there is no way of tracing the genetic background, beyond Jenny herself. This must be a hard thing to bear indeed. But meeting this serene young woman, with all her understanding and strength, so much of which must have come from her parents' special care, I thought to myself that she would cope, and cope well.

'Always competitive, my mum,' said Kerry, looking across at Jenny with a smile. 'I remember she was so determined that I was going to win this fancy dress competition, and decided that I was going to go as the Golden Goose, complete with egg! I sulked all day wanting to be a princess. There was a princess there who looked so beautiful, everyone said she would win. Mum dressed me up in bright yellow tights and a horrible goose's outfit she had spent days making, and I had to hold a golden egg to show the judges.'

She smiled mischievously at Jenny.

'Anyway, I was sulking but she was so determined that I was going to get first prize. And I did. I still can't believe it. The hours she must have spent on that costume.'

We all laughed, and Connie rolled over on her back at our feet and wagged her tail over the red and white snooty foxes on the carpet. This is a famous carpet, a magnificent dark blue with its cartoon foxes, their noses in the air, dolled up like huntsmen with top hats. It was one of the more bizarre reasons why Jenny and Geoff fell in love with the pub, and it has become an attraction in its own right, like Connie.

All around us were pictures and posters of Connie, but here, at our feet, the real thing stretched out again with a grunt and went back to sleep. She had obviously been for another walk with Jenny after the hectic rush of Sunday lunches and was covered in mud. She was so dark against the dark blue carpet that one could hardly see her. I once trod on her paws walking into the pub from the bright sunshine outside. Mortified, I bent down to give her a hug and was rewarded with one of those gentle little licks which are so much Connie's 'specials'. She's very forgiving.

The conversation turned to other childhood memories, and Kerry reminded her mother of the awfulness of trying to translate messages on the telephone when they were children.

'So many family rows about that!'

'What happens when the person at the other end doesn't have a minicom?' I asked.

'It's so embarrassing,' said Kerry. 'You have to talk as though you are talking to your mother. That's what they tell you to do. It is no good saying, "Tell her I love her", because they will repeat exactly what you say. You have to say "I love you" to some shadowy operator you've never met.'

Jenny, lip-reading, shook her head vehemently.

'No, No! You just have to forget the operator's there and talk as you would naturally. It's easy when you get the hang of it.'

Her determination flashed through. She told us about the first time she rang Geoff's mother, with the minicom being translated through type-talk. The operator on type-talk had typed to Jenny, 'She's crying at the other end.' The emotion of the first time that Jenny had been able to 'speak' on the phone had been too much for her mother-in-law.

Jenny now has a portable minicom which she can carry around with her like a mobile phone. Given to her by her employers in Blackburn, she says it is wonderful. She can even 'talk' to people from a public phone box or an emergency phone. It is useful in any eventuality.

Jenny now told the story of trying to find me that morning so that we could take the pictures, and I realised with a shock that for her it had been quite different. She thought I had disappeared and forgotten her, and even came right back down to see if I was in the car park. And she was reluctant to make Connie face yet another car journey. Why hadn't I thought of that? I knew how much Connie hated the car. Nevertheless, our mutual affection for each other, and our shared humour, iron out these misunderstandings. Oddly this has enabled our friendship and respect to grow in a touching and quirky way. We have both learnt from those mistakes.

Geoff, looking tired, came into the bar to open up. Jenny had just been saying how much support he has given her over the years and how she wanted to make sure he understood how grateful she was.

'He has never stood in my way. Whatever I have wanted to do, he has stood back and let me.'

I remembered their son Adrian, when asked what difference Connie had made to Jenny's life, saying that once they always had to keep tabs on her, worry about her, that sort of thing. Nowadays they never know where she is. That's the difference.

Geoff unlocked the pub door. It was time for me to go. They had their work to do: meals to prepare and the bar to set up. Even in the depths of winter, on a cold night, they would be packed. This once was a sleepy pub in a quiet little village. Now, thanks to Geoff's and Jenny's hard work, and Connie's too, the pub is buzzing summer and winter and they are run off their feet. Lunchtime had been a nightmare, especially as the vegetables were late.

Kerry said goodbye and gave me a hug. They are a very tactile family. A lot of that must be to do with Jenny's deafness. I was so glad to have met this beautiful young woman and had been so impressed by her, as I had by all the family. Kerry's understanding of deafness made me realise that here was a bridge between our worlds. She had quickly grasped that Jenny and I were trying to make this book a bridge of understanding, and that our friendship too had been the first of many bridges for us both, despite all our misunderstandings of time and place . . .

I gave the snoring Connie a last stroke. She banged her tail, but didn't open her eyes. It had been a busy day!

Kerry said as I left:

'Connie has made possible the simple things that hearing people take for granted—a doorbell, telephone, alarms—and, most importantly, she makes Mother's invisible disability a visible one.

'People see Connie and love her, and automatically know Mother is deaf. Connie breaks the ice and works wonders for Deaf Awareness. So now I am redundant. I am no longer needed to tell Mother the sounds that are being made. She is independent—at long last!'

She paused and gave me a warm smile.

168

'Mum told me that the most important thing about the book is your friendship. It means a lot to her.'

I felt tears start up in my eyes and once again I had that warm feeling.

'Yes,' I smiled, 'I feel that way too. Jenny is always going to be special to me now . . . We'll always be friends.'

There, beside me, suddenly, was a dark shape. A cold little nose was pushed into my hand. I felt that delicate, warm lick which is Connie's speciality, so different from the enthusiastic tongue-lashing I get from my two labradors.

'Please don't forget me, either,' she seemed to be saying. I bent down and gave her a stroke. She wagged that fronded tail and looked up at me. As if I could ever forget her! We had shared so much these past months, the three of us. And Connie . . . well, Connie is just Connie, gentle, dedicated to Jenny. Just Connie. Unforgettable. She'll always be special to me too.

An artist's impression of how the new centre could look

HEARING DOGS FOR DEAF PEOPLE

'Touch and Tell Appeal'

At the time of writing, the facilities which Hearing Dogs for Deaf People now have in Lewknor and North Yorkshire can no longer cope with training the number of dogs needed to meet the growing demand. Neither of the centres can be extended, and the charity has had to look elsewhere for an expansion programme which would provide sufficient amenities not only for the dog training, but for all the other departments necessary for the goals to be achieved. For example, the puppies' socialising department needs to be enlarged, and office administration, public relations, fund-raising, after-care services and accommodation for recipients and students on training courses, as well as facilities for education and staff training, are all necessary requisites for this rapidly expanding charity.

Hearing Dogs for Deaf People could not have achieved their present success without their loyal supporters, and today they need this support more than ever. The waiting list for trained dogs is up to 18 months and rising, but this could be cut by half with the opening of a third training centre.

With this in mind, Hearing Dogs for Deaf People have launched the 'Touch and Tell Appeal '97' to raise the million pounds needed for a new centre, and have recently purchased what they hope will be the ideal property to meet their future requirements—Grange Farm, a sixteenth-century farmhouse set in 27 acres of Chiltern countryside. It has an extensive range of farm and stable buildings already in existence, providing the opportunity for conversion.

All donations and enquiries about the appeal for a new centre can be addressed to:

Hearing Dogs for Deaf People
The Training Centre
London Road (A40)
Lewknor
Oxon. OX9 5RY